THE
DRUMMER'S
PATH

The Circle: earth, sky, dance, music. Gregory Ince, John Blandford, and Obara Wali Rahman perform Wedding Lamba at Lincoln Center, New York, 1977.

THE
DRUMMER'S
PATH

■

Moving the Spirit
with Ritual and
Traditional Drumming

■

SULE GREG WILSON

Destiny Books
Rochester, Vermont

Destiny Books
One Park Street
Rochester, Vermont 05767

Library of Congress Cataloging-in-Publication Data

Wilson, Sule Greg.
   The drummer's path : moving the spirit with ritual and traditional
drumming / Sule Greg Wilson.
     p. cm.
   Includes bibliographical references and index.
   ISBN 0-89281-359-8 (pbk)
   1. Drum—Instruction and study. 2. Afro-Americans—Music—Instruction
and study. I. Title.
   MT655.W56 1991
   786.9'089'96—dc20
                                        91-29373
                                             CIP
                                           MN

Printed and bound in the United States

Text design by Randi Jinkins

Cover photograph: Kimati Dinizulu plays the Gome drum. Orisa Festival,
New York City, 1986. Photo by Sule Greg Wilson.

10   9   8   7   6   5   4   3   2   1

Destiny Books is a division of Inner Traditions International, Ltd.

Distributed to the book trade in the United States by American International
Distribution Corporation (AIDC)

Distributed to the book trade in Canada by Book Center, Inc., Montreal,
Quebec

Anetch hrauten, paut Shepsu, Neteru. Tua-u.

To my parents, who gave me life and let me live my path.

To Uncle Hugh, who taught me being yourself and always growing.

To Ray and to John: teachers of the Spirit. You showed me how to see and how to harmonize.

To Baba Ngoma: your forbearance and discipline enabled me to survive the rest.

To Shekhem ur Shekhem, who gave me the hookups and made me stand as me.

To Nana Yao Opare Dinizulu, without whose decades of work this book would never have been accepted.

Baba Ifakorede: your presence is in all drummers here.

Also thanks to: Jim Huffman and Mary Yearwood of the Schomburg Center, for your help in acquiring images for the book; Mai Tefa Angaza, for your encouragement; Montego Joe, for airtime, and good vibes; Oswald Simmonds, Jr., Marilyn Nance, Roy Lewis, Vanessa Thomas-Wilson, and Hakim Mutlug—for your artistic and photographic talents; the people of Shinnecock, Long Island, for your welcome, time and again; Chief Bey, Shekhem ur Shekhem, the Dodsons, and friends—for reading drafts and drafts.

Urr Pesh, sweet sweet; you've lived all this with me. You are circle to my cross, the temper on my heat, the earth about my air. Tua Neter. Kheper.

Shepsut Kemkem TchetTer: Shekhem em Shepsu-t, tua-u. Be!

Suddenly, performance became ritual as the priest, Richard Ahye, was possessed by Shango. Orisa Festival, New York City, 1986.

Sensitive

I *feel* the Orisa coming.

I mean, at Bembes

When the drums are right
and the dancing's tight
and the clave is pumping and clear and bright

There's a sudden interior wind, and the air and my guts start to
tingle/contract,

A vibrant, sense-heightened awareness becomes and:

ZOOM!!! the Gods they fly, fly through and by.

Incandescing a bit of **me** into the ether....

Aspiring to harmonize,
Striving to grasp the meaning.

And be One with the Power
And the Flow.

The Cool One watching all
Can take the heat;
Steps forth and allows me to see my path.

And in the jamming basement throes
of rhythm passed out to the world
Spirit comes
and takes a horse
and passes Truth to all those gathered.
I listen.
I see.
I learn.

Contents

Babatunde Olatunji dances his Ngoma. *Orisa Conference, New York City, 1986.*

FOREWORD

Time is the Great Resolver of all things. What was once feared is now accepted, even sought out. Today we are witness to a tremendous change in people's attitudes towards an instrument that has played a tremendous role in the traditional ways of many cultures the world over. I speak of the drum.

This was not always so. Many Christian missionaries to Africa mention "loud discordant notes played on the drum" in their diaries. Because of this misperception of percussion, the drum was relegated to the background in most Western musical renditions and compositions. And, because it allowed long-range communication prior to the invention of the telegraph and telephone, the drum was banned from use by early African inhabitants of this American land.

The Drummer's Path is a significant contribution toward understanding the role that the drum has played in the history and lifestyle of African people at home and those brought to the "New World" generations ago. *The Drummer's Path* reminds us that Africans came across the waters with more than one instrument, and that these music and Spirit sciences were used to continue the African celebration of life and sense of unity under strenuous (to say the least!) circumstances in a strange and foreign land.

This well-writtern and well-documented book about the drum—and the drummer—contributes much toward a better general understanding of the instrument and its evocative power. *The Drummer's Path* illustrates for us the position the drum takes and holds in the life of those who choose to play it.

Sule Greg Wilson outlines the approach necessary for each individual drummer to become one with her or his instrument. In a very precise way the author gives us insight into how to access the voice and power of the drum. He shows us, through his life story, the sacrifice and discipline crucial to all who care to learn how to play and understand the instrument, whether one drums for entertaining, thanksgiving, or healing.

This book shows us: Yes; there is a Spirit in the body of the drum carved out of the trunk of a tree; there is a Spirit in the skin of the drum itself. All this, plus the Spirit of the person playing the drum, becomes an irresistible force against any immovable object. Practice, persistence, discipline, and continuous search for and study of the culture—as revealed in festival rhythms and chants and music dedicated to the different natural forces, or deities—will help the student to discover what makes one a drummer, or a master drummer.

I highly recommend *The Drummer's Path* to all who are involved in the field of creating a better understanding and appreciation of a rich cultural heritage, that of African and Diaspora percussion. It is a thorough study and a great contribution to the knowledge of the drum and of the drummer.

Babatunde Olatunji
New York
January, 1992

PREFACE
THE CALL

Music is sacred. It is an integral part of the Way of Life of many traditional cultures throughout the world; it is the invocation of vital energies that ensure a community's survival. Music helps maintain harmony in and with both the visible and invisible world.

The poem "Sensitive" on page vii describes my experience as a participant in Afro-Cuban religious ceremonies (a *bembe*), imbibing their power. Yet, because I had not been "made" in the Yoruba church, I would/could not fully dissolve/absolve myself into God's faces as delimited by that ceremony. Watching the happenings, taking in energy, it was tough to not let go, but respect and protocol demanded I stay steady on the rhythm I was playing on the bell: *K-chink! Chink, k-ching-ching, Chink! K-chink! Chink, k-ching-ching, Chink!* By playing in a *bembe*'s drum ensemble, I was involved in a system of "energy management" that modern motivational tapes, etcetera, are but a sterile dilution of. Unfortunately, the prejudices of today hold the wisdom of the traditional world at bay. You see, in the modern Western world, traditional ritual and ceremony are often trivialized. Outsiders view sacred acts and the cycles of observances as childish superstition or as simple diversion, an exotic treat imported for a passive audience. Non-Western classics and folklore are merely a commodity, touted, at best, as a "source of inspiration" for accepted (Western) artists or, at worst, perceived as a novelty ripe for exploitation.

Despite these narrow perceptions the power of music to tap one's emotions remains unquestioned. Listen: after a presentation of Western "classical" or pop music, the acculturated audience speaks of being "moved" by the performance; in fact, to be touched, to "be one" with the performance is lauded as high art.

Now, extend that principle beyond the confines of the anonymous concert hall. Take it to a down-home church service, or a bembe, where the music, the words, the movement extend themselves into the minds, the bodies, the souls of everyone present and you breathe, you perspire, your eyes bat, and you tingle in your toes or in your palms or in your belly or your crotch and you don't sit still, you've got to MOVE! The music's with you; you've got the Spirit. You have been so moved. Spiritually "touching" the attendees of a service—"performance," if you will—is standard in a non-Western religious context. It's part of what you go to service for. And it's not just African; it's not exclusive. Tapping into one's emotions is utilized by all people: dervishes and playwrights. Then why is it that when these techniques are used in a non-Christian religious context they are suddenly something to fear and are branded "primitive superstition" or "voodoo"? What it really is, is its own science, one thousand years old, a molding of the powers of imagination and Spirit, formed by art and forged by discipline, passing through the vehicle of the artist to the vessel that is the audience—an audience that is all too often, in the Western context, an unknowing participant subliminally seduced by unfocused emotional/spiritual energy.

Even today, after generations in the West, the tradition of the "everyday, yet sacred" continues. Many famous and powerful performers—Aretha Franklin, Billy Wilson, Sam Cooke, Chief Bey, Daniel Ponce, Celia Cruz, Sister Rosetta Tharpe, and Take Six are examples—were steeped in the world of ritual or the church prior to embarking on their stage careers. These "folk" utilize that spiritual performance foundation to get their secular "thing" across.

But it ain't about "doing your thing." With mastery of the techniques of "moving" others comes responsibility. Artists and musicians are manipulating power in the form of mood-altering sonics and information coded in iconic form—colors, patterns of line and movement, garments and images. Therefore "performing" becomes much more than just having fun, more than a night's gig for earning daily bread—there is a consciousness, a spiritual and social awareness that must be adhered to.

With this power, just "touching" someone emotionally and intellectually isn't enough. Do you wake a slumbering friend for no reason? Woman and Man have observed and studied for thousands of years to learn just what it takes to alter their own or another's state of consciousness. Let us learn from them, the traditional world's masters of sound and movement. Reinventing the wheel is the long way around. Let us use God's first gift to us. In art, as all else, the first tool is one's own self. As the Sphinx said: "Know thyself."

Whether it is acknowledged by the culture at large or not, artists affect people with much more than technique and training. They do it with who they are, with their emotions, with their life experiences, with their thoughts. One's state of Spirit molds the music and the art that is made, and it affects the people it comes in contact with. Your words, your thoughts, your work are charged with your cumulative and instantaneous Being. That's why in some African societies it is against the law to "talk bad 'bout somebody." Understand this truth. Because what you think and feel becomes your world.

Making the music, U.S. style. The Usonium, a new set of drums developed by the author (above) and James Cherry, has steel shells and only a small sound hole opposite the goatskin head. The size and materials of the Usonium allow the drum to complement conga, djembe, and other drum orchestras and techniques, without losing its distinctive sound.

Why & How: An
Autobiographical Sketch

ello. Hetep. 'S hap'nin? In doing art and music and history, searching for something not based in ignorance or falsehood, some basic principles of how harmony and spirituality manifest in the everyday and the particular have come clear for me. What you now read is my endeavor to share those revelations with you. In fancy terms, you have in your hands a plea for the inclusion of generic principles of traditional music and spirituality into the purview of musicians, performers, and all folks who live. This book started out as two one-page essays written by me about a month apart, in February and March of 1981. The first one spoke of how vital it was for drummers to also be dancers. The second spoke of the need to be centered with both your personal talents and your legacy. After the essays were down on paper, I wrote out a checklist of things I'd come to understand in my years of drumming that I wanted to share with folks who found themselves traveling that same road. There are stories in this book that describe the instant of revelation for me; I've included examples of times when these principles came into action in my life; I share times when I've felt Spirit's hand at work, and what of that I've grasped; I hope the anecdotes open the way to help you getting some insight, too.

Music is hard to talk about; this goes for drums especially, because they are so much a real-time experience. When a rhythm is being played you feel the beat, the authority of the drummer, the *receptivity* of the instrument, and it gets you: sometimes below the diaphragm, sometimes below the navel. Wherever it hits you, you feel it instantly. There's no need for the translation of words.

So we can say that, first and foremost, drums are not of the intellect. A drum is a mantra machine, something whose vibrations interact with your own to effect a change. At this point, I suggest you put on *The Drummer's Path* audiocassette/CD (sold separately) and let that play, to set the mood and clear the air. Listen to the children, the heartbeat, the chanters calling the "Opening of the Way." And, of course, listen to the drums: instruments from different cultures calling forth the same principle—saying "still the mind, drop preconceptions; grow." From cacaphony you distill the truth. Now let's go over what you'll find in this book.

"The Call" you just read was written to remind people of how powerful our own thoughts and preconceptions are. As one of America's "tough-guy" icons once told his just blown-to-smithereens boss: "A man's got to know his limitations." If you don't, you're strolling on the edge of a cliff, wearing a blindfold. The autobiography (where you are now) tells how I developed into the person who could write this book—it details the worldview that shaped my perceptions—so that the experienced Truth behind the Principles will, I hope, be clear to you. The historical note (chapter 2) is vital, in that we can't go forward unless we know where we have been and recognize what it is we've carried with us all this time. The Principles themselves are simple and clear. There are twelve of them; it just worked out that way. Read the Principles and give them a chance, don't dismiss them. Try them on and out for yourself. Don't say, "This stuff is so simple I'm not going to use it!" I've already made that mistake, and had to follow someone else's path, instead of my own. Remember: simple and easy are not the same thing. "Health and the Drummer"? Well, to do it right you've got to be fit, and every true warrior also knows how to heal. As for "Women and Traditional Drumming"—I've heard so much woofing back and forth about how women are supposed to be and aren't supposed to be, I thought I'd share with you some relevant research that I and some others have done on the subject. The afterword puts into context and perspective all that has gone before. And, for the edification of the reader, there is a glossary of—I hope—all the obscure terms used in *The Drummer's Path*. If it's still unclear, let me know. I'll get back to you on it. Following the glossary is a selected bibliography for those who would like to read more on the subjects presented.

That's it; a journal of a journey never done. A drummer's path. Peace, y'all. Now let's move on.

One of my favorite photographs is a snapshot of my paternal grandfather, my big brother, and me. My mother's handwritten note says it was taken about 1963 out in the backyard of my childhood home in Washington, D.C. All three of us have on silly hats, and Chico—my brother—is clowning around with the old ukulele that's been in the house from time immemorial. Already taller than Pop-Pop, my sixteen-year-old brother has on the straw hat Daddy wore in some play and his long head is cocked to the side, lips pursed in concentration as he works to strum a chord.

Our Geechee grandfather is turned away from the lens; he looks back at his first grandchild. Wearing a much-abused World War I officer's hat that belonged to my maternal grandfather, Pop-Pop is softly smil-

Photo by Mignon Gregory Wilson

Already an interest in percussion: Pop-Pop, Chico, and me. Washington, D.C., 1963.

ing, and his hands are resting on my bony five-year-old shoulders that don't even come up to his belt buckle. In my hands are the bongos that Chico brought home when I was about three years old, I guess to keep the ukulele company. My head (in a trounced gray felt Confederate cavalry hat) is bowed—I don't even see the camera—my attention totally focused on those drums. I'm already absorbed into them, just five years old.

Before I was big enough for the bongos I beat on oatmeal boxes. They were kept in the kitchen, in my toy-box space beneath the cupboard. After numberless crushed box tops I learned to get at least different, if not good, sounds out those things. I had a good time.

I had inborn interest in percussion and the luck to be born into a household of intellect and Spirit. I've got artists and writers on both sides of my family, and spiritseers and palm readers and such, too. I was taught to be proud of my Madagascan, Manding, and Choctaw self at the same time I heard about my Euro-American great-great grandfather, Judge Wilson, down near Lake Greenwood, South Carolina way, and the big-time Hancocks of Austin, Texas. I was given awareness of my strengths and of my family.

I saw what pride can accomplish, both personally and nationwide. In the early and mid-1960s, just about the time that photo with my grandfather and brother was taken, changes were sweeping the world. The British and the French empires were giving up the ghost of overt control. Africa, the Caribbean, and Asia were becoming decolonized and demanding Western-trained native citizens to take the place of European bureaucrats. Folks from all over the world came to study in the States. Many enrolled at Howard University in Washington, D.C.; so many, in fact, that Howard became the traditionally black college with the nation's largest foreign-student population. My Philadelphia-born father's job (director of foreign student services) was to assist these students from the melanized world during their stay in the U.S. of A.

To spotlight its multicultural makeup, Howard University instituted, as part of its annual homecoming celebration, an event called International Night, when students from other countries could present their national and traditional folk and royal lore to the general student body. Part of my father's job as director was to organize this foreign-students' showcase and just generally make sure that International Night was a success. At home, salting his meatloaf, he'd describe the different national personalities and recount the travails of coping with people who were brought up under the French system, or the British system, or seemingly no system at all. It was great dinnertime fare.

Despite the backstage clashes and intercultural confusions, International Night became a reality every year. And there I was, down front, watching as students from Guinea, Ghana, Nigeria, Cameroons, Mali, Trinidad, Kenya, India—you name it—wore traditional clothing and sang traditional songs and played traditional instruments, showing pride and independence.

And knobby, riney me, I soaked it up. As those internationals strutted their stuff before peers and their professors, I saw the right thing, done proud.

Years pass. It's the late sixties—1969. It's Friday evening and I'm home nearly alone (my parents are out at a State Department dinner, big brother Chico's away at school, and my big sister Wendy's Malian boyfriend is visiting, so they're out of my hair). By this time I'm in my junior high school's African Heritage Club's dance troupe: the Oya African Dancers and Drummers. I've got a conga drum in the house, and Mommy and Daddy are out, so I just bop and bop and bop and bop away.

My playing is banging through the walls, so after a while Wendy and Mouktar come into my room to watch and to talk. Mouktar is impressed with what he hears; he says I should study, I should go to New York and work with the people he knows there. I listen, but I don't believe him. At least, I don't seriously consider his suggestion. Somehow, I have the presence within my twelve-year-old mind to tell him "No thanks, I've got too much studying to do yet." Precocious.

Junior high school was my first real chance at independence, rebellion, freedom! I took it. I dropped my preadolescent interest in science; instead I became an artist, moving away from the preferred family vocation, intellectualism, to embrace the unspoken impetus, my bloodline's secret passion: creativity!

The Afro-American History Club at Rabaut Junior High School had spawned a dramatic arm in 1968, the year before my arrival. By the time I entered junior high the club had folded, but the Oya African Dancers and Drummers, the social offshoot of the club, had survived. My Aunt Jean, a math teacher at the school, was cosponsor. Under "Muga's" beneficent rule I was able to have a social life (and still be under family observation! so much for real rebellion . . .) and focus much of the

This flyer from 1973 was posted at the sandwich shop near Banneker Recreation Center, where Oya once rehearsed. It documents the work Oya did, and with whom, and has added value because it was signed by members of the company: Paka, Ama, Okola, and others. It was during this performance at the docks that I heard the voice of the ancestors.

inborn talent and bubbling hormones I had, as well as some of the intellectual Afro-consciousness stuff I had soaked up at home listening to parents, siblings, and elders.

Through Oya I got my first paycheck, my first girlfriend, and my name, "Sule." Here's how the name came to be:

I was up against a wall, literally. Marcie and Donna were all in my face, Okola and Soyini stood as backups. Muga's truncated classroom on the second floor of Rabaut Junior High School never seemed smaller.

"So, what's it gonna be?" demanded Donna, the elder McQueen sister, pulling up to her full height. She still had to look up into my eyes. Marcie (my soon-to-be girlfriend) blocked my escape with jutted hips and arms akimbo.

Slowly, deliberately, deliciously, I reached inside my Army-surplus knapsack, pulled out the caramel-colored, dog-eared book, and handed it over to "Dowse" (Marcie).

I cleared my throat. "There! Where the paper is. On page seventeen." Having got what they wanted, the sisters all retreated, clustering around Calvin's desk to check out the marked page in Names from Africa. *I had pored over that book for three days, from Wednesday rehearsal until now. Last night, sitting at the kitchen table eating sugar-frosted flakes, I'd made my decision.*

"This one?" Soyini squeaked, adjusting her black-oval-framed, inch-thick lenses again. She read it aloud. "Sule?"

"Sule, huh? What's that mean?" Muga put down her red marking pen and swiveled out from behind her desk. "Lemme see, lemme see." She leaned forward; the girls withdrew. Muga read out loud: "'Sule. West Africa. Meaning: adventurous.' Haw! Haw! That's a good one. Yep, that's you, Sule, all right." She smiled. Me, from the wall, I checked everyone's eyes. Yes, they accepted it. "Sule—adventurous." That's me! It's true!

Through Oya, I made friends, and I got to see the Senegalese National Dance Company when they came to the United States in 1972. The skinny little boy with the bongos was finding his road.

The next year, 1973, at the City Docks in Annapolis, Maryland, my ancestors burned their life force into my soul.

Oya had performed at the Village Festival of Black Arts and Crafts the year before. Smelling salt air and dancing hard on wooden cobbles, the wind whipped our singing and drumbeats away. This year's festival, better advertised and better attended, had a portable outdoor stage, a sound system, and I had my crew of new friends from Wilson High as part of Oya now.

The July Fourth sun was hot, despite the sea breezes moving up through the Old Town. The Oya African Dancers and Drummers rolled in from D.C. in the open bed of a blue Ford truck, playing cowbells, liberation-colored congas, and chanting at the top of our lungs. Sliding through narrow streets and down steep hills to the dockside Festival, turning all heads—black teens in wax-print and country cloth, blue jeans, and natural hair—we sang "Power to the People! Black, Black Power to the African People! Who will survive in America? Very few niggers and no crackers at all!"

After unloading the truck and setting up for the show, there was time. The women looked at wares. We fellas, on stage in the summer sun, behind the mikes, started messing around: talking street talk, acting real jive, every now and then quoting a Funkadelic line. I made a *ssssuck!* noise in the microphone; then I suddenly felt that I was not alone. "What are you supposed to be representing here? You came with a mission, and the message is clear: are you going to be a sweet-talk stagefront man, or will you help all People, give them power through your hands?"

I took in breath, stared. The fellas were still giggling; no! I felt this! I really could not believe it; in my guts, in my head I heard this voice, telling me, showing me to straighten up my act. I took my gaze out: sitting in a lone folding chair was my cousin Alan, the politically conscious one (he drove the truck that day). In his presence I saw, I heard, I felt my family, my people, all truth in that silent inside voice and face before me. I took it in, let out breath. I left the mike, the stage, and waited for the show to begin.

Now research indicates that some of my ancestors were imported through the port of Annapolis.

It was a time of change. Oya's influence couldn't weather my absorption into the high school scene, but my interest in percussion did. Jamming in D.C. parks, I met Dominicans and Anglos who played serious music. I made the Wilson High School yearbook my sophomore year, with a drum between my legs. A new, independent step had been made.

I arrived in New York City in 1977, transferring from Oberlin College in Ohio to New York University. I had made trips to the Apple before. It had what I needed. In the summer of '75 I had run up on the train with my best friend Ronald, on the prowl for art and Hendrix memorabilia — we also snuck into Sly Stone's wedding reception after watching the ceremony and performance at Madison Square Garden. Another time I drove up with Steve (Ama-from-the-dance-group's boyfriend). He had demo tapes to give to Funkadelic. I brought my drums. January of 1976 (my winter term project from Oberlin) was spent studying with Babatunde Olatunji and Kehinde Stewart at the old second-floor studio on 125th Street in Harlem, where masters such as John Coltrane, Ladji Camara, and Chief Bey performed. I was accomplished enough by then to "hang out with the big boys." Techniques I had painfully practiced back in Washington—studying with Baba Ngoma (every Tuesday and Thursday night from 7:00 to 10:00, for two years of high school) and with Tunda, Oya's drum leader—began to pay off. I performed with Olatunji that winter: three drummers—Olatunji, Kehinde, and Sule. And Ms. Aquasiba Joan Derby leading the dance.

When Mongo Santamaria came to Oberlin just before I transferred out, I worked my way backstage and talked to Steve Berrios, Mongo's drummer, about my aspirations. I got his number and as soon as I arrived in the Big City—June 1, 1977—I called him. Within two weeks of leaving Ohio I was studying with the ace students of Ladji Camara and Chief Bey, now part of the International Afrikan-American Ballet: Okulose Wiles, the Ince brothers, and Neil Clark (Harry Belafonte's percussionist). I was drawn to them and to their attention to authentic detail. Look at the photo of them on page 10, taken at one of the International's shows at Klitgord Auditorium in Brooklyn, New York. You can see they're making good music; strong and dedicated. Again, as in D.C. on International Night, what I saw was the right thing, done proud.

I worked with International for five years (1978 to 1982) dancing, drumming, videotaping, stage lighting, writing, and doing research. I also branched out, going to Boston to perform with the Art of Black Dance and Music, studying tap with Miss Eleanor Harris and Charles "Cookie" Cooke. Vanessa (my Hollis-raised Trini/Gullah fiancée) and I learned lindy hop from the Sullivans (George and Sugar) and Mama Lu Parks. I sat at the feet of African-American elders: Ray McKethan, Chief Bey, Eleanor Harris and Jean Blackwell Hutson (both my distant cousins I found out), Ali Abdullah, Pepsi Bethel, John Bubbles, Joe Carrol, Edith Wilson, C. Scoby Strohman, and the Copasetics. I taught at the African Heritage Center in D.C. and other such things. I got a bachelor's degree in television production, and a master's in history and archives. In 1981 Vanessa and I married, doing *Lamba* as sweet rain fell, pouring libation to the wondrous past and to our unknown future.

Spirituality is part of my heritage and part of my household, my coming up. I heard stories of hauntings and visitations, and I knew how to leave my body and come back, when I wanted. The world is more than we see, I was told. Part of my openness to this reality was having folks from other cultures stay at our house, and having friends who took me to

Photo by Sule Greg Wilson

The right thing, done proud: the Ince brothers—Walter and Greg—on djembe, Neil Clarke (right) on jun-jun. *Notice the* kutiba *(full pants) worn by the musicians. Klitgord Auditorium, Brooklyn, New York, 1978.*

Photo by Vanessa Thomas-Wilson

Backstage at City College after our show—the Copasetics and International's male dancers. Standing (left): Charles "Cookie" Cooke, Bubba Gaines, Charles "Honi" Coles, James "Buster" Brown; squatting (left): the author, Gregory Ince, Clyde Wilder, John Blandford, Oswald Simmonds, Jr.

temple and mosque and church and ashram and. . . . I was searching, looking for Truth, content beyond form.

Drumming and meditation came together for me in New York City. I pored over books at the Tree of Life in Harlem and Weiser's in the Village. That gave me intellect. A start. But then, by playing for bembes on the weekends, listening to elders from the United States and to artists when they came over from across the waters, and experiencing juju from The Homeland firsthand (that's another story), the pieces of the spiritual puzzle (that was the true foundation of everything I had been learning and living through) began coming together clearly.

Ausar Auset Society's priesthood training provided a Kabalistic framework that zogginated (as we say at home), my gumbo of experiences. I became able to recognize the ancestral push that coagulates, that permeates, my life. I came to perceive the power of "the right thing, done proud."

And so this book, a distillation of my experiences as drummer, dancer, folklorist, researcher, and priest-in-training. There is power and truth in each of the Principles stated herein. They have all been proven by experience, brought forth and made clear through the Light of the Supreme Being.

Don't take them lightly. I have seen what people can be if they are in harmony with them, and how they are if they ignore them. Any of them. Don't cheat yourself, or deny anyone else the healing that you could give them through work done well. 'Cause that's what it's all about: Make Power, and Change the World.

Photo by Sule Greg Wilson

Part of Hetep (living in harmony) is respecting those who came before. Pictured above is the shrine to the Egun (revered dead, the ancestors). Orisa Conference, New York City, 1986.

<u>ONE</u>

RHYTHMS AND
SELF-IDENTITY

The more music I learn, the deeper is the significance to me of asking and answering, "Is this the way it's s'posed to be?" Striving to get it right has become my prayer to the ancestors. But true, accurate information on a particular rhythm is very, very hard to receive. I have found, and read, that traditional musicians are leery of divulging to inquirers the secrets of their religion and the music that makes up a vital and powerful part of that religion. Remember "The Call"? This science of music is something that changes people's consciousness, and it's nothing to take (or give) lightly. An equivalent would be to ask a priest what he or she does in confessional or when administering the Host, or what the Mason's symbols are about. Or what a psychiatrist does, or how to do brain surgery.

Aside from people's reticence to divulge information, there are other factors in the difficulty of getting the lowdown on drumming. For one thing, it depends on whether the person you are questioning is from a family that traditionally holds such knowledge or whether this person received it as training for a theater production. When you hear "Stop, or I'll shoot!" in the streets, it's different than in a movie or a play. And someone's real wedding is different from one on TV. It may look authentic on the tube—with beautiful lacy gowns, an organ playing "Here Comes the Bride," and sniffling witnesses—but if you've been through it, you know there is a completely different vibe, in reality.

I found that out the hard way. After my uncle the judge performed the civil service in Philadelphia (my father's hometown), we had the ceremonial service in Queens a week later, on the lawn of the house where my wife grew up. It was a misty, blessed-with-the-signs-of-Oshun Saturday. . . .

Wedding Lamba—for real. Vanessa and I, ritualizing our union before our gathered families. Hollis, New York, 1981.

Photo by Mansa Musa

I looked around. Okay, Greg and Ozzie are in place, djembe *and* songba *shielded from moisture by the open-sided, yellow-and-white tent my grandmother-in-law insisted on getting (good thing! with this morning's showers). Let's see, the Sisters have done their part with the lucky leaves, and the rain's almost let up. . . . Oh, oh; John's got that* serious *look on his face. . . .*

"GIMME THE BREAK NOW; I THINK I CAN!" It was time. Out we stepped, bubas *flowing, faces raised to the kissing rain. My attending Brothers, John (elder) in the lead and Clyde behind, escorted me through the circle formation that brings the groom out, front and center: Wedding Lamba was under way.*

I'd done this dance over and over again, in community centers, in the street, and in concert halls. The choreography—lines, circles, solos, and back steps—is simple but precise. Gregory and Ozzie are rockin', standing under the yellow-and-white awning of the lawn tent, keeping the drizzle off their drums. Everything's normal, just as before. It's a show.

Then I look up: my mother. Despite the stroke, she's taking it all in, deeply observing, glowing with pride at her son's stepping out, and craning to catch the unfamiliar ceremony. Daddy's head is bobbing with the music. My gaze shifts; everyone is watching, raptly watching: eyes locked, brows intent. This "show" is for real!

The women's voices stream up in chorus, the music insists, and here comes my bride, sashaying out from behind the tent: shoulders tight with nerves, face aglow with love.

John and Clyde step out, right on cue, and hold, waiting for me to come, too. On my bare feet the sodden grass is cool, and slick with rain. The Guyanese caterer is hanging out the kitchen window, smiling. The men, the women are standing, waiting. Everyone is watching! I'm not breathing! Come on! Take it in, push out, take it in. . . . I swallow, blink my eyes. I find my limbs, and I step forth to sweet and sweet and dance with my new wife.

The performance had become ritual. It became real life; there is a difference.

Other factors also impinge on getting the "goods" about percussion. The skill of your "informant" (anthropology's term for someone who shares knowledge of their culture with you) as a teacher—that person's proficiency with your language and ability to transmit knowledge to someone else—are major considerations, as is your sensitivity to the sacred aspect of the topic.

Before attempting, as an artist, to imbibe another's culture, there are questions you must answer about yourself. Are you grounded enough in your own sacred music and folklore to reach a common ground? Can you play gospel tambourine, sing a blues lick? Do you know the classic tap steps, did you ever lindy hop, or bop, or do some kinda hand dance with your mamma and poppa? What did your people do in the Old Country? Or back on the down-home farm? Knowing where you come from keeps you safe and centered, like a trail of bread crumbs or twine, when you're delving in the realm of another.

Photo by Sule Greg Wilson

Balogun leads the Chuck Davis Dance Company's drummers. New York City, 1978.

All God's creations have power. To use power in Hetep (peace and harmony) you must accept yourself—your past, your culture and its contributions. *Then* you can bring them to the world, to help you learn the world. If you don't, you will always be searching, trying to fill up that hole in your soul, made when you ignored who you are.

I once heard a story about Balogun (G.R.H.S.) when he went to West Africa. A lead drummer for the Chuck Davis Dance Company, he had been around the African scene for years and had received much exposure and experience in traditional African drums and ceremony. When he finally crossed the waters and got back Home, he played and played, sharing his knowledge of "the Culture" with his brothers in the Motherland. They were impressed. They nodded, and smiled appreciatively.

And when he was done, they said (politely, through their interpreter), "That was very good, what you have learned of our traditions. But tell us," they asked, "what do *your* people do?" He had no answer.

It's like pushing past your mamma to get a hold on her grandma.

Sometimes lessons come in reflection. I've learned mine, too.

It came through the grapevine: Sekou Toure, the president of the Republic of Guinea, was to visit the United States! Everyone wanted to see him, and all the New York area African/cultural dance groups were dying and vying to perform for him when he came to the city. A reception was scheduled at the Harriet Tubman School in Harlem, and the group I was with, the International Afrikan-American Ballet, was on the bill to perform. Boy, were we excited! Here was the symbol of African nationalist resistance, from the land of Les Ballets Africaines! Here was our chance to show how much love we have for our homeland and for the independence that President Toure represented.

We made sure we were ready: rehearsals, costume checks, rehearsals, libations, rehearsals, prayers, and rehearsals. Yeah! We was ready! And we was down!

Photo by Sule Greg Wilson

As part of International's Finale, out comes MFOA (Message From Our Ancestors). Klitgord Auditorium, Brooklyn, New York, 1978.

Came the time. We danced and smiled and jumped and sweated and performed on that tiny, dusty little junior high school stage and gave it all we got. We watched him have some interest, clear his throat, and politely smile.

In past years I've reflected on that: what we did, how we got to be there, who did and didn't get to dance on that stage. . . .

Where is our power? Not in being imitation traditional Africa. The purebloods've got us beat. Cold. Any day. (If they continue to honor it.) Nor is our power in being American, though it is a good diplomatic defense in the world as it stands today. That's a reality, too.

Like it or not, U.S. Africans have been changed from the stay here in the States; no denying it. But Spirit *never* left! Close your eyes, breathe, listen; it's right here. Look at what John Mason, Nana Ansah, Bobby O'Meally, Sterling Stuckey, St. Clair Drake, Pearl Primus, Shekhem ur Shekhem, Nana Dinizulu, and Oba Osergeiman all have done. They create the world each day. What has James Brown had to say? And everyone of us, Sweet Honey in the Rock?

So, what we could have done for the Manding president: do his stuff as good as we ever could, but also pull out all the stops and be sure we do ours, the thangs that the whole world wants to learn: that old-time combination of African spirit and city-lights, streetwise Harlem jive. Shoulda given him some classic lindy and tap, and topped it off with some new street rap and break-dance steps. 'Cause there ain't nothing he can say to that. 'Cause that's us, Money, and that's what it be like. Do you follow what I'm saying, Homeboy, Girlfriend? Spirits Sing, as Spirits Will.

TWO

HAND DRUMS AND THE U.S. SOUND: HISTORICAL POINTS

When it comes to overt, straight-line continuity—in form and content—of specific West African cultural manifestations, it seems that U.S.ans are at a loss. There is no organized Shango religion, as in Trinidad—Shango being the name of a Yoruba deity (see photo on page vi). Spiritual leaders don't greet each other with "as-salaam," as in Brazil (carried over by Muslim Manding). U.S.ans don't have people named Kofi, Kwame, Akua, and call their roots work by a particular ethnicity's name for it.

Nevertheless, there are subtle carryovers. One is the tradition of choosing African-sounding names for children—names like Keisha, Peabo, Shaquala, Tinisha, Bobo. Some names and words are direct African holdovers, like Bubba, okra, and cooters. African-Americans still throw *wanga*. African-Americans still have the Congolese gesture of patience and restraint; art historian Robert Farris Thompson notes the way this was captured by Henry O. Tanner in his 1894 painting, *The Thankful Poor*. U.S. Africans still hold religious meetings where folks "talk in tongues" and "get the Spirit," communing with the other side, as Africans always do. (See Mickey Hart's *Drumming at the Edge of Magic* to learn what happened to the Spirit Possession folks.) And African syntax, the taking of European words and putting African grammar, inflection, and rhythm, and therefore different meaning, on them, pervades the world by way of U.S. pop culture, you dig?

U.S. African culture expresses itself in zoots and pegs, too. A handbook of Harlem jive, 1944.

U.S. Africans transformed much. Across the Atlantic, back in Africa, everyone's lives were tied in with doing right by God and working with those people who were charged with carrying the Spirit. Then look at the preacher, man or woman, in America. Harriet Tubman manifested the Spirit in visions. George Washington Carver, when asked, would say that all he "derived" from peanuts and other plants was told to him by the plants themselves; he was in touch with the Spirit of them. There's the example of Dr. Susan Smith McKinney-Steward, an African-American woman who became a homeopathic M.D. in 1870 and was organist and choirmaster for her church for nearly thirty years. She stood by Spirit. What about the ministers El Hajj Malik Shabazz (Malcolm X) and Martin Luther King, Jr.; Adam Powell, Sr., and Adam Powell, Jr.; and Nat Turner? Those are all leaders—manifestations of Black Power—coming straight from the Spirit. Nothing more, nothing less.

Nonmelanized people living in what became the United States knew about that power. In South Carolina they lived with it and feared it. They experienced the power of the Spirit-calling drum. That's why in 1740, after the Stono Rebellion, the South Carolina colonial assembly outlawed hand drums. In some areas Europeans were outnumbered by Africans five to one. (And don't mention the Native Americans.) With the across-the-miles communication that talking drums gave Africans, those who rose up against slavery and utilized that technology stood a good chance of success. To destroy that military power, Europeans said drums—all drums—had to stop. The law was: You play, you lose your hand. Maryland, then other colonies, quickly followed suit with similar "no-drumming-in-public" laws.

But Africa didn't stop. Until the 1820s (only five generations ago—your grandma's grandma) African masquerades took to the streets in upstate New York and New York City for "Pinkster Day," celebrating with drumming, song, and dance. Pinkster, a corruption of "Pentecost"—the seventh Sunday after Easter—was the day the Holy Spirit descended upon the Apostles. This celebration of Spirit Possession as recounted in the Good Book was a week-long ceremony in which a governor or king of the blacks held court, commingling with the Native Americans and reaffirming their heritage. (For more on this celebration see Stuckey and Holloway, listed in the Bibliography.) And everyone knows the Santo Domingo and down-home mix that took place at Congo Square in New Orleans, the birthplace of jazz. In fact, so many West Africans lived in eighteenth-century Louisiana that Bambara (a language from the land of the djembe drum—Mali, Guinea, Sierra Leone) was named the official Creole tongue.

In the 1930s Amer-Africans told government interviewers from the Works Progress Administration about doing their rituals with hand drums. How did they do it, if drums were outlawed? Simple: take your everyday mortar or water barrel, put a rim and a skin on it, and there's your drum, anytime you need it. And, for safety's sake, it was instantly dismantlable. Others buried their drums in the earth after use.

Let's look at some other documentation. In the British Museum is a drum, acquired in Virginia and part of the Sloane Bequest of 1753 (Sir Hans Sloane's collections became the nucleus of the museum). The British believed it was an Indian drum. They were wrong. It is an Akan drum. It looks like an Ashanti *apentemma;* but this one was made of American cedar and deerskin. Carved, roped, and decorated in tradi-

Made from American cedar and deerskin, this Akan drum was collected in Virginia before 1753. For years mislabeled an "Indian drum," this instrument is proof of the continuation of African material culture over here 'cross the waters.

tional style, the drum is material proof that Africans kept up their musical and ceremonial traditions in the land that was to be the United States. Since there is no documentation on the drum's use, we can infer that the Africans were able to keep their customs secret. Was it called an "Indian" drum because the collectors assumed that only Indians would be able to produce such an artifact? Or was the drum perhaps gathered at a Native American settlement? If this were so, it would affirm the belief that Native Americans supported the continuation of traditions among the imported Africans.

The Akan drum gives evidence of African drumming in North America in the mid-eighteenth century. Let's look to the end of the nineteenth. Once when leafing through the sheet-music collection at the Schomburg

Center for Research in Black Culture, I came across a "Camptown Races" lyric book, published in New York by McLaughlin Brothers. In the final scene, way in the background in the bleachers, beyond the "Zip Coon" and "Mammy" stereotypes, are two musicians in clownish outfits. On the right is a banjo player, to the left, a drummer. The drummer is playing a field drum, a European instrument. But what matters is *how* he's playing it, and with what.

Field drum, Euro-style, is played with two sticks, and with the drum heads parallel to the earth and sky. If you're an old Mali *songba* player or savannah *brekete* man, you'll do as the guy in the illustration did: play the drum transversely, across the lap. And you'll probably use a curved stick, as the Camptown accompanist did. You might even use your left hand to dampen the sound on the drum's other head. Look at the illus-

Sheet music cover for "Camptown Races," c. 1900. The costumed drummer (background center) is playing his field drum in African style: transverse, left hand muffling the tone, and with a curved stick.

Capoeira *was used against slavecatchers. Played to music, Europeans thought the Africans were just dancing, not practicing a deadly martial art. Notice the* berimbau *(one-string bow) to the right. Eighteenth-century engraving.*

tration—it's all there: that black drummer is playing that European military instrument in perfect African style.

You see, the Spirit never left. Folks invented ways to do what they had to right under the oppressor's nose. Take Brazil's *capoeiristas:* they turned the Angolan martial art of *capoeira* into a dance; then there was no problem. Owners liked to see happy, dancing slaves, so what could be more innocuous than the men dancing and sparring in a circle? Hey, if you don't hide it, it can never be found. Listen to "The BaKongo Samba" on *The Drummer's Path* audiocassette/CD for the *berimbau* (used in *capoeira*) and other traditional African and African-American instruments. If you believe that Africans in the United States were willing to give up their cultures, reflect on this: the only place in the West where it was decreed that Africans could not play hand drums was the one place where they came up with foot drums—tap dancing, that is. It's dancing and drumming, all in one, the way playing trap drums is being a traditional drum ensemble all by yourself. U.S. African society wasn't smashed to nothing, it was just condensed. What does that mean to today's people? It means that into the feet is where the Spirit, the African vocabulary of Spirit-calling, went to. Ask your elders on this side of the Atlantic—the old-time jazz drummers—where they got their rhythms and the answer will be as from any other African musician: they watched the people carrying the Spirit—the dancers—and played what they saw coming at them.

Drummers, listen: when you want to be inventive, don't just go on what you think you know. Get the rhythm from the dance, from those speaking the forces of the Gods with their bodies. External circumstances can bust up any drum, but no one can break up the Spirit that makes you dance.

Picture this down on the old plantation: a spiritually in-tune Sister's walking back from fetching water down at the well, and—BOOM!—Spirit comes. What do you do to help out? First, get somebody who talks in tongues. Then, tie down a skin on the old slop bucket or grab a rice-pounding mortar; quick as a flash you've got yourself a drum and you're

From the Abby Aldrich Rockefeller Collection, Williamsburg, VA

Jammin' in the Quarters: The Old Plantation *painted in the mid-1700s. Once again proof that Africans held their own. Note the drum, similar to the Yoruba* gudugudu. *The banjo, though a four-string, has the short drone string, or chanterelle, refuting the allegation that the drone string was added by Euro-American Joel Sweeny around 1840.*

The drummer's inspiration: high steppin' strutters gettin' down. Jitterbuggin' in Clarksdale, Mississippi, 1939

Photo courtesy of *down beat* magazine

Baby Dodds, master jazz drummer, c. 1940. Compare his stick technique to that of the drummer depicted in The Old Plantation.

ready to jam, playing and complementing whatever the Spirit—through that Sister's body—is saying.

Look to history: who were the innovators, who set the standard for drumming in the United States? Not Buddy, pal. It was Baby. Baby Dodds, King Oliver's & Louis Armstrong's rhythm man, the master of "double drumming": playing snare and bass drum with sticks alone. His mother's granddaddy played "talking drums." It's about using the voice. Think: why *have* a drum set? Development of such a polyrhythmic instrument is not the European way. Traditional Euro-drumming is identical: twenty people playing the same *purrr-rum-pa-pum-pum*, or, in another scenario, just one *bodhran* or tabor player. African drums play in parts that combine to make a melody, just like trap-set drums are played, or like a Low Country hand-clap ensemble.

African aesthetics, using Western tools: Gertrude "Ma" Rainey (Bessie Smith's mentor) and her Wild Cat Band, including "Gabriel" on drums and Thomas A. Dorsey, father of gospel music, on piano; c. 1923.

Here are the parts, traditional orchestra to trap set, one-to-one: you've got the bell player in the trap set's cymbals; baby drum in the high-hat; bass in the foot and floor toms; *sekere* and lead drum in the snare and foot pedal. Even the most pared-down drum set has the three parts for the three basic drum voices: the snare's the top; the cymbal's the middle; and the bottom is in the foot. The choice of these specific voices is part of the African aesthetics maintained by Africans here in the West. No matter what the form or the type of Afro-derived music you choose, it's all hooked up the same way. Electric slide, merengue, go-go, or samba— same thing. *The Drummer's Path* audiocassette/CD features various hand drum techniques on "Hometown," side 1 ("Essential Drums").

To get an idea of the early U.S. African sensitivity to playing differ- ent parts, listen to recordings of the old jazz bands, Dixieland, and ragtime music as performed by King Oliver and Louis Armstrong. In those groundbreaking (or should I say "crossover") ensembles, each musician has his or her own part to play—and keeps that part—despite the fact that what that person is playing is cutting across the other parts and the basic melody while he or she is doing it. Fantastic!

To experience the difference between Afro- and Euro-aesthetic playing styles, listen to a recording by Paul Whiteman or some other Euro-American jazz band, then check out some swinging sides cut by James Reese Europe's "Harlem Hell Fighters" jazz orchestra or Clef Club men recorded just after the Great War. If you've only heard Whiteman and his peers, you will be left with the wrong impression for sure. Imagine James Brown done by Muzak. *Jazz* is supposed to be dance music, to be functional, invocational. It was designed by God to make you dance, to "forget your troubles . . . get happy . . . [and] get ready for the Judgment Day." That fills the bill for functional and spiritual, *n'est-ce pas?* Besides, what does the word "jazz" mean? To say to someone you're gonna "jazz 'em" means you want to sex them up, you want to jump their bones and do the Wild Thang. What am I saying? The music is made from primal energy. Jazz is more than improvisation: it is reproduction, resurrection of your downtrodden soul. See Robert Farris Thompson's *Flash of the Spirit* or Albert Murray's *Stomping the Blues* for more info on that.

Look at it demographically. The music is called "Dixieland" because "way down South in Dixie" is where nearly all the Africans in the United States lived, up until the "exodus" of the teens, 1920s, and 1930s. Those African diaspora musicians played their clarinets, violins, jugs, and tubas with their continued "back home" aesthetic: with the feel and the orchestration of the drum. Listen to some Congo drums for how the parts talk, how they interact. Or the juju music tradition of Nigeria. Put European instruments in the hands of Africans and they arrange and play them to fit their own traditional orchestral sound.

For verification, come back across the waters to Dixieland and listen once again to a group such as King Oliver's Creole Jazz Band, featuring Louis Armstrong or Kid Ory's Original Creole Jazz Band. That ain't no oompah stuff, no straight-up-and-down way of playing, even if the work is done on a German-made horn. That "raggedy time" style, with all them people conversing at once on their instruments, could only have been created through the Spirit. Anybody else'd get mad at being talked over.

This playfulness with meter and tempo dovetails into other areas, as well. You know that break dancing came out of music ensembles all dropping out, save one rhythmic instrument. In that ensuing "break," the dancers would pull out their best stuff and really burn. This sense of stop-time, break and jam, has been around as long as Africans, it seems. Listen to Robert Farris Thompson in Joseph E. Holloway's *Africanisms in American Culture:*

> Cable had noted that the great, or bass, drum was beaten in Congo Square with "slow vehemence," whereas the smaller drum was played "fiercely and rapidly." The full complement of instrumentation included a four-string banjo, and for a spell all the other instruments would drop out while the banjoist expounded; then there would come a cry of "yeaaaaah!" and then the crash of drums, horns and rattles.

Sounds like the stuff I grew up on: going to church and James Brown and Gloria Lynn bein' real and P-Funk and the original Sky Church and boot dancers and drum corps and "Jingo" and what have you. Which brings us to where we are today: talkin' Africa on American soil through European tools, words, and instruments. No matter what the vehicle, Spirit's the same. Think about that, and riff on it.

Gettin' up for the downstroke: New Orleans' Re-Birth Jazz Band's Second Line. No matter what the vehicle, Spirit is gonna manifest. Orisa Conference, New York City, 1986.

Photo by Sule Greg Wilson

THREE
THE PRINCIPLES

Y ou know, I never stopped to ask myself, "Can I drum?" When the time came I did it. Before Oya, before classes and jam sessions and 'shedding in my bedroom with the headphones on, I did it.

One springtime Saturday afternoon I found myself in a quiet second-floor loft, with sunlight, silence, a cowbell, and a conga. And I played them.

The first time I played, that first time, I heard only myself. I cast my Spirit against bare walls, a high ceiling, and a wood floor that bounced my sound right back to me. I heard my heart beating; breath. I heard the room, the echoes of percussion, power loosed. I heard me. That day was when this book began.

The Principles started revealing themselves then, with music coming through me in an empty room, as my big sister worked below on an outdoor mural. I heard *my* voice, and all my other music has come through that. The Principles recounted below are aids to centering oneself in the music, to humbling oneself to the realization that every-thing has its moment—but never two things at once—and that in harmony there is peace, and vice versa. Read on.

1. BREATH

For an internal combustion engine to run at peak performance, there must be the proper fuel/air mixture. Oxygen must be present to unleash the gasoline's power. The same principle applies to the human machine. The carburetor—your rate and efficiency of breathing—must work at its optimum level, if you want to do your best.

Therefore, your breath must be deep, regular, and always controlled. Deep breathing imparts oxygen to all your bronchia, so that O_2 gets into your blood faster. It keeps your body relaxed so your arms and hands can efficiently perform as needed. And regular breathing accomplishes two vital things.

First, it hooks your body's cycles into that of the music you're doing. Breathe with the music's tempo: in through the nose, and out through the nose or mouth. Controlled breath yokes you with the sounds you're creating and gives you steady access to your body's power. I found this out the hard way:

Children's squeals, the biting smell of chlorine, and gold-tinged sunlight came from the open window behind me. Boy, did I need that late-day, late summer breeze: those drummers were good! Three "vets"—they were already shaving! and handled the duffel bags on their backs like masters—had come sauntering into Banneker Rec right after Oya's Friday evening rehearsal. Modibo and Audie had already caught the bus up Georgia Avenue, so I was the only one left to answer the question: "Was there some drummers playin' around here?" I looked at them, bulk-muscled, in bell-bottoms and fatigues and dashikis and shades and Afros out to here and . . . I cleared my throat. "Yeah; we . . . , Oya rehearses here." "You wit' them?" asked the red one, the short one in the middle. "Um-hum." "Well all right, let's play." He reached for a folding chair.

The three unslung their axes: two Mexican congas and one gon bop tumbao. I unpacked the Company's red-black-and-green spray-painted conga and watched as the elders set up four chairs. They sat me down: trial by fire.

Guaguanco in a circle of four; they had me playing a fast "gallop." [Guaguanco is featured in "Mundu del Espiritu" on The Drummer's Path *audiocassette/CD.] These guys were cool—broad shoulders, fast hands, and secret smiles as they kept pushing and pushing and pushing the tempo up! The music got faster, and faster, and faster. I could feel my muscles starting to burn. This was tough enough!*

I pulled my arms and upper body up, and up, trying to press ahead, to keep up with the pace. My purple "wet look" T-shirt was more than just looking *wet, and I was panting. How did these Brothers do it?! Looking around all calm, not busting a sweat, totally relaxed. . . .*

Relaxed! They're relaxed, their breathing is slow and cool and they . . . Hey! That's it! The breath!

I took a deep inhale, then another, trying to sync it with the music. In . . . and out . . . and in . . . I swallowed, then noticed I was hunched over. I straightened up, tightened my guts, shook my head and . . . .

Suddenly, my breathing dropped to half-time; I was instantly cooler. Holding that tempo was suddenly, literally, no sweat. My shoulders naturally unfolded from their hunched-up position, my chin came off my chest, my spine uncurled. I was relaxed, and now able to keep up, comfortably, with the other drummers. It was, as I would have said at the time, far out. Somehow, instinctively, I had tuned-in to a secret of the body and the breath, and it had saved me. I could hang with the big guys, this time.

When I started playing old-time banjo I found I had to employ the principle of breath again. The basic technique—hit a note with one fingernail, brush all the strings with all fingers on a downstroke, then sound a note on the drone string with one thumb—was simple, but deadly. At the Old-Time Banjo weekend in Berkeley Springs I watched and watched and watched it done. After some practice my right hand learned the stroke, got the "feel" of it. And suddenly, I was rocking. I was deep into it, seriously practicing. The other students near me on that West Virginia hillside had completely faded from my sphere of awareness. Even the morning-cool rock I was sitting on was suddenly far, far away. All I knew was the "note, strummey, drone, strummey, note, strummey, drone, strummey" exercise I had been given.

The feel for playing the instrument that was coming to me was almost reggae, but with swing time added up front. I could hear it in my head, but it wouldn't translate to my hands. I bobbed my head to make rhythm, and almost lost it all. That shouldn't have happened! I tapped my foot; that didn't help. Then, I slowed down the pace, and found the problem. I was out of synch between "note, strummey" and my rate of breathing.

I had to break it way down. As I reined in the tempo, my chest shuddered, breath shallowed even more, then fell into pace with the music.

FRANK LESLIE'S
ILLUSTRATED
NEWSPAPER

No. 1,463.—Vol. LVII. NEW YORK—FOR THE WEEK ENDING OCTOBER 6, 1883. [Price, 10 Cents. $4.00 Yearly. $2 Months, $2.00.]

VIRGINIA.—A NIGHT SCENE IN LYNCHBURG DURING THE TOBACCO SEASON—NEGRO TOBACCO-FARMERS MAKING MERRY.
FROM A SKETCH BY C. UPHAM.—SEE PAGE 107.

Banjo is also a percussion instrument, slapping the drone and popping strings. Check out the bones man's technique; playing two-handed is African style. Also see the illustration of Khamitian women percussionists on page 98.

I uncurled from around the instrument, straightening my spine and raising my head. Yeah! Drone, strummey, note, strummey, on! It was just like drumming! The timing of my breath allowed me to relax and speed up. If you're out of synch, it's like nails on a chalkboard. If you're in, it's like cool satin bedsheets. Breathe on.

That was reason number one for good breathing: relaxation. Reason number two for good breathing: Your rate of breathing determines where your sensitivity and spirituality reside while you're playing. If your breathing is high in your chest, fast and shallow, ain't no Power gonna come. You are heating up your head, constricting your sphere of awareness. You are hyperventilating. You can hurt yourself, faint, or break a blood vessel, breathing like that. What *should* you be doing?

Go to church. Watch the folks when Spirit hits them: breath first comes in shudders, spasms; then it slows, and cools the people down. What you're witnessing is the changeover to Spirit, lower-chest breathing. It's the natural way. It's how a little baby, the most relaxed person we know, breathes: from its navel.

Go to a *bembe.* How does Obatala (see "Ausar" in the glossary) breathe? So cool, so slow, so beyond the world. The person carrying him is open to what God has to say and do *in* the world. The drummer's job is to *make* receptivity come and sustain it. You can't do that if you're panting like a dog.

Changing your rate of breathing is like shifting gears. At the usual rate of eighteen breaths per minute you're in drive. This rate of oxygenation keeps you relatively tense, focused only in the here and now. You can maneuver down the street, but you won't tune in to Spirit.

Twelve to nine breaths per minute is the optimum rate for physical exercise. You stay relaxed and clearheaded, and you have the oxygen you need to efficiently fuel your body.

Drumming calls for intuition, sensitivity, a circularity to your touch and your energy. If you are breathing slowly—say, at the rate of four to six breaths per minute—your powers of intuition and harmony with the music and situation have a chance to manifest.

Respiration is another word for breathing. You "re-spirit-ate"—put the Spirit back into your body. And when you get an idea, you get Inspiration! "In-spirit-ation," the spirit of that idea comes *in.* So, when you re-spire when drumming and search for in-spiration, you aspire to achieve, in your body, that slow, cool cycle of breathing. Better than liquor, it works every time.

2. GOOD POSTURE

The poem that opens this book says, "There's a sudden interior wind, and the air and my guts start to tingle/contract. . . ."

What I'm feeling and referring to there are the "wheels," the chakras—those energy centers in your body that instantly know of new vibes in the room. Everyone has experienced that: somebody comes in, or something is said (or not said), and you just get a feeling, the atmosphere has changed. . . . Your chakras are the receptors of these changes in environmental energy.

Just as there is a circulatory system for blood and its nutrients, so there is a system of channels for energy. Directing this energy system is what acupuncturists do. Needles, heat, or pressure are applied to a person's skin to affect the energy channel, the meridian, beneath. Where

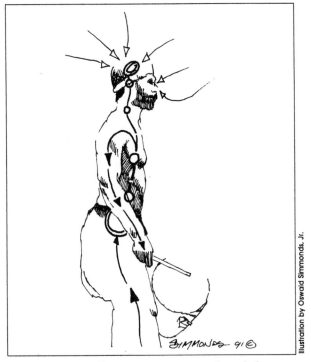

Illustration by Oswald Simmonds, Jr.

For proper energy flow, yang energy enters through the crown chakra (top of the head), the pineal (between the eyes), and the nose (breath)to the lower tan t'ien, then up and out into the arms as needed. Yin energy flows up the legs from contact with the earth.

major channels compound are the chakras, the energy "crossroads" of your body. Chakras are also the liaison between the physical, electromagnetic, and spiritual bodies of humans. It's deep. Get some acupuncture done; it'll clear your head.

As liaison, the chakras are also receptors of energy from outside, as when Spirit comes at church, or at a performance—or at temple or the woods or a lake or some intimate setting. Spirit comes in through chakras. Feel it for yourself, next time.

This is all necessary to know if you are going to run your vehicle, your body, and not let it run you. To get optimum performance you've gotta put in hi-test and keep the injectors of your living machine clean. The energy has got to be flowing to be of any use. If you're hunched over while playing, it's the same as putting a knot in a garden hose. If you're straight-backed and relaxed, though, you maximize the energy flow from your root chakra/lower *tan t'ien.* There's no place for a traffic jam in the control centers. It's simple; it works.

There is another "secret" of energy flow, which I first got from reading *The Teachings of Don Juan: A Yaqui Way of Knowledge* by Carlos Castaneda. As part of his initiation into being sensitive to the energy of the world around him, the author of the book was told to keep his arms and hands in a certain posture when walking. In order to do this one has to strive to maintain one's equilibrium a certain way—which, I believe, was the real lesson. Well, that was the insight I got when I tried it.

You've got to "massage" your root chakra, down in your pelvic girdle. The pumping of your legs as you walk is like two sticks rubbing, making heat, and that heat is what turns that jazzy "wanna-do-the-nasty" energy into something that can flow more safely through the body's chakras and meridians. Through mind and energy control your *chi* is sublimated to more refined energy. Likewise, if you are standing while playing a drum, always keep your knees flexed just a little, so you can bounce, and rock with the music. You try it and see. It should pump up the heat. Let me know what happens.

Here are some more reasons for being conscious of and implementing good posture. If your back is straight:
• Your arms and shoulders can be relaxed for playing.
• You allow the free flow of energy.
• You can breathe slowly and deeply.
• You can observe the dance, and whatever else is before you, without strain.

Walter Ince—half Cuban, half Panamanian—demonstrates proper djembe stance at Ile-Ife Day, Philadelphia, 1977.

If your knees are flexed:
- You are free to move in any direction, as need be.
- You can subtly bounce, an action that regenerates your energy.
- You are relaxed, not "locked in" or "uptight," which would impede receptivity.

Your feet should be parallel, about shoulder-width apart. Don't stand flat-footed. It doesn't work for a boxer, it won't work for you. Stay on the balls of your feet. You know, you shouldn't be flat-footed when playing sitting down either. Let's go through some practicalities.

When seated:
- Let the drum rest in the cradle of your inner thigh, calf, and foot. It doesn't matter which drum, unless it's supposed to be free standing.
- Don't clench the drum between your knees like your thighs are a vise. You're cutting off your circulation, creating undue strain on your internal organs, and deadening the sound of your instrument.
- Lean it to one side, to allow sound to come out of the drum. Be sure to practice playing leaning it to either side, otherwise you'll favor one set of muscles and get lopsided.
- Sit on the edge of your chair; give energy outward as you receive it from the ether above and around you. Use your body as a soundboard or baffle: let the sound come from the drum, bounce off your chest, and flow on to those before you.
- Rest the drum on the ground, not on your feet. Ouch! I see people do that all the time; isn't it painful?
- If you're playing *djembe,* get a strap! The drum was made to be hung.

If the drum is in your lap, the above still applies: stay straight. When your lower back sags, so does your energy. A curved spine creates energy blockages that strain you to overcome them. You might say, "Well, I'm doing all right now." That may be true, but you're making your work harder than it has to be. You should be able to lean comfortably forward and backward, as the need arises, to stretch muscles, to rock with the music, to have fun, and stay in tune.

I've heard that there are specific positions for specific *djembe* rhythms. My experience shows that some positions are more conducive to playing certain rhythms, depending on whether the emphasis in the rhythm is on the right or left hand. Perhaps certain postures are in themselves *mudram* (energy-focusing body positions), helping the body to be a certain *yantra* (sacred line pattern). It's like turning your body into a *veve* (a sacred, invoking series of lines from the Voudoun tradition of Haiti and Dahomey).

I have also found that certain playing positions aid in "locking off" certain chakras. This enables the player to "dam the river" of energy and place or direct it where one desires. And when you're playing fast and furious, that's a blessing.

3. PLAY AMBIDEXTROUSLY

Many players, particularly when starting out, favor one side, one hand, usually the right, over the other. This is not good. Catching accents from a dancer or singer is always awkward if their beat falls on your weak hand. Besides, balanced playing also evens up muscular and nervous development and exercises both sides of the brain, necessary for an equilibrated psyche.

Sometimes you can tell what hand a drummer favors, just by looking: one shoulder may be higher (from carrying the drum on one side only), one hand may be bigger, more calloused. This can mess up your spine and lead to complications later in life.

There is also a "higher," spiritual reason for even-handedness. If you favor one side of your body, you focus more energy to the other side of your brain, and you are going to get polarized toward left (rational, scientific, reasoning) brain activities or to right (intuitive, artistic, feeling) brain activities. If you're polarized you tense up—the last thing you want if you are striving for efficient, accurate, and intuitive playing. The goal is to be centered/equilibrated in your body and spiritual energies and not be too hard/stiff (or soft/loose, either). Don't be too yang or yin, too masculine or feminine. You don't want to be an intellectual robot (yang), but you also don't want to be so "into it" (yin) that you don't pay attention to what is going on around you, and you lose focus, the rhythm, and face.

An equilibrated state of spirit takes diligence and hard work to achieve. And part of the work to reach that state is using both of your hands equally. If both your hands work, then so do both sides of the brain. This necessary equilibration is symbolized in mythic pairs: the vulture and cobra on King Tut's death mask, by the dove and the serpent of Western mystery systems, and by the moon and the sun of the Hindus (Ha Tha). Or you can see it in the paired thunder stones of Shango, in the Taoist yin/yang and in the caduceus of Hermes/Mercury seen today in the logo of the American Medical Association.

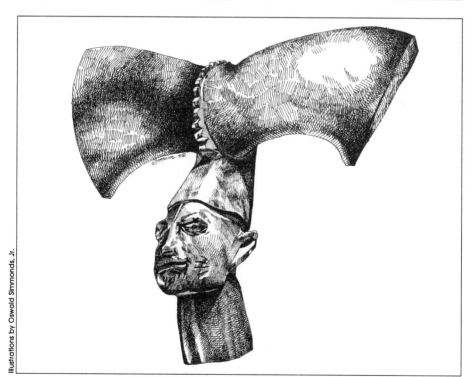

Illustrations by Oswald Simmonds, Jr.

Icons of the equilibrated brain: the caduceus, the Uraeus on Tut's brow, Shango's thunderstones.

In practical terms, you cannot be a leader if your head is not on straight. To be correct you must follow the Golden Mean and ease on down the Golden Road.

This advice has a mechanical, practical side, too. From time to time in performance you may be called upon to switch, to play a part from the other side of the rhythm, picking up the slack from another person's part. It's all so easy with ambidextrous playing. If you're standing in the middle, a step to either side is no big thing.

4. SING, DANCE, AND PLAY EQUALLY WELL (AND SIMULTANEOUSLY)

Yes, it does sound tough, but there's good reason to be able to do it, and no good reason not to. To invoke the music, it's got to be inside you. Your body, mind, and spirit have to be able to function "on automatic." Your hands play the part while you concentrate on the song, or the upcoming change in the music, or what the *orisa* is saying.

Application of this principle isn't difficult. It just takes practice. Pull out a record of Santeria music and your cowbell, or just your hands, and play or clap the clave as you sing the songs. Listen to "Iron and Steel" and "Mundu de Espiritu (Spirit World)" on *The Drummer's Path* audio-cassette/CD for the appropriate clave. Then, practice the deity's signature dance steps while you're singing and playing or clapping the clave. (For information on the dance steps, write to me at the address given at the end of the book.) At first you may fumble, but soon come, people, soon come. With the ins and outs of the orchestra impressed into your muscles and nerves, into your spirit, by moving with it, you can "rock-and-roll" with it all night long.

To achieve the ability to "rock-and-roll" with the music, whether the full orchestra is there playing or not, you must "digest" the rhythm into your own soul, into your spirit. Your *nephesh, ka,* electromagnetic body, your blood and aura, all have to strum (or "note, strummey") with the beat.

How does one make that happen? Move with the music. Don't just dance to it; dance *with* it. Chant the chants, learn the steps, tap your feet to the music you be making. That's the ticket. That's the only way inside the rhythm, inside the music. As in the kung-fu movies—the acolytes and masters don't think about the next move; they've practiced that move, every other move, and any variation to and from it a million times, in rhythm. After time, all the possibilities become instinctive. Or, as in *capoeira*, new steps and parries come through from the Great Darkness and appear as needed, instantly.

Here's an example of someone's need to know where and where not to rock the music:

Doing the back step; now I can check out the audience. The toddler in the front row reminds me of my daughter, bouncing in Momma's lap like a trampoline in response to the drums—but Mommy doesn't notice 'cause she's all into Malika's solo: coming upstage it's kick, kick, take your arms the opposite way; kick, kick, kick, kick—she's doing that step over again waiting for the break—hey, that means I'm next!

The adrenaline comes on high. I pull my breathing down and slow and visualize how we did the changes in rehearsal last night, but this time it's for real. She kicks, and I scoop air in my barrel turns. Keeping the edge of the stage in peripheral vision, I wait for the characteristic KRAK! of Greg's djembe drum as he marks the moment I transfer my momentum back into the air, as soon as I make contact with the linoleum-covered cement stage floor. KRAK! KRAK! KRAK! KRAK! I hear the "gimme-the-time-now-I-think-I-do!" break, and I spin out into my first step, taking straddle jumps up beyond my co-dancer's heads.

Malika's out of there, and I step in, launching into the torso-parallel-to-the-floor-arms-perpendicular move that I love so much ' cause it feels just like you're flying, and I'm UP!, touchdown, UP!, touchdown, UP! . . . WHAM! "What?!" "What!?" Flying through the air, I'm looking around. WHAM! Somebody else is playing the lead and is marking my jumps on the bottom, their drum's energy is knocking me, pushing me into the floor, not snapping me back to the air! What happened? WHAM! Again! My stomach knots. It's not Greg, what's going on here? He's switched off playing the lead with Taiwo! WHAM!

In shock, I cut it short. My feet hit the floor; I spin and stop, stop dead in a deep crouch; pull back my warming breath. I look: I wait for Taiwo's eye contact; let's start again, together. Jump, step! Jump, step! Jump, step! Jump, step! But again, he's not with me: flams and rolls are popping indiscriminately. It's pretty to hear, impressive to the audience, but out-of-synch pain to this dancer. I change to a simple "one, two, one, two, one, two" step, and from that he marks me on time.

Photo by Vanessa Thomas-Wilson

Dance, as drumming, is timing, coordinating your energy to fuse with the music and your colleagues to create harmony. IAAB flies through their Finale, 1981; the author is at right, back to the camera.

> *Taiwo, who came up under Olatunji and then, through circum-*
> *stances, floated free-lance for so long, never got the chance to dance,*
> *to find that coordinated place in his soul.*

Drummers, musicians, singers, writers, everybody: to know, to really *know* what you're playing or saying is all about, get out from behind your axe and dance. Be experiential, more than intellectual. Feel for yourself and in yourself the rhythm making you move; it will impress your spirit far more than watching, and when you have to play it and make other people move that way, you will be able to. You'll *know* when somebody else is playing right, or when they be shuckin' and jivin'. 'Cause when it's good, it sinks right in, gets stored in the "memory banks" of your *nephesh*, where it can be called up and out to help others—drummers, dancers, chanters—to deep down "get that feelin'."

5. KNOW THE CHANTS AND LITURGY

Traditional music—ritual, social, performance—is designed to impart a complete experience, to create a particular "atmosphere." To play the music correctly, you have to know what that atmosphere is. Listen to "BaKongo Samba" on *The Drummer's Path* audiocassette/CD. It's not just the rhythm that's good, it's the song on top complementing it that makes the complete musical experience. (Too bad you can't see the dancing, too.)

The best singers captivate you not just with their singing technique, but with their acting, their emoting skill; they go into the meaning of a lyric and invoke its "feeling" with their own *chi* force. They fine-tune their raw, primal energy into emotional states ("vibes") and transmit it to the audience through their voices and their attitudes. Do the same with your instruments whatever they may be.

When playing traditional music, this can be done only if you honor the Creator and respect Her/His vehicles: the people and the tradition that put together the music you're trying to do. Perform it the way it was intended. If there are lyrics to be sung or words to recite—and there often are with African music—know them, word for melody.

Knowing the melody helps the drumming, for African music always has points of interaction where the curves of melody and rhythm are parallel, then suddenly tangent, or even become one. The melody and rhythm push and reinforce each other, just as father and mother do for the child, their product, their offspring; greater than either alone.

Musicians, you must be able to sing as you play. And not mess up. Doing this, you are tied, locked in with the chanters around you; you are sensitized to the progressions, the changes in your ritual or performance. Singing locks you in with the other musicians, who also chant. It gets you into the groove, invokes the energy/spirit within you, and "locks" the breath of the chanter with the timing of the music and the dance, as all inhale and exhale as one. If you listen closely to some of the ensemble pieces on *The Drummer's Path* audiocassette/CD, you can occasionally hear the musicians humming and moaning and chanting as they play. Through this they are "locked into" the music.

Chanting is good for you; it sets your insides to humming. These internal resonances massage your body's organs and stimulate your energy centers (chakras) and energy channels (meridians). Certain vibration rates (mantras) stimulate your glandular system (pineal, pituitary, endocrine). Naturally occurring psychochemicals (endorphins) are then released into your brain and body, which are then the proper environment for a supraphysical experience. Which is what you, as performers, are trying to do for your audience, your co-performers, and yourselves: send 'em home feeling good. Needless to say, artificial stimulants get in the way.

Some traditions use chemicals found in nature: the shamanistic tradition is one of these. Often a feature of male-focused/left-brain cultures, the use of peyote or other substances is a technique to force the chakras into a receptive state. Sometimes pain (see the film *A Man Called Horse*) or externally induced sensory deprivation (as in the movie *Altered States*) or starvation or dehydration are used to induce the release of psychochemicals. Why? Let's look to culture. Most societies can be classified as male- or female-focused, or perhaps, male-focused and egalitarian. The West, for the past 4,000 years or so, has been about reducing the feminine in its social systems. One theory that seeks to explain this is the concept of right brain and left brain dominance. According to this model, the reasoning, segregative (left brain) tendency has led to the exclusion of women from many niches of society, including places of power in the culture's religious system.

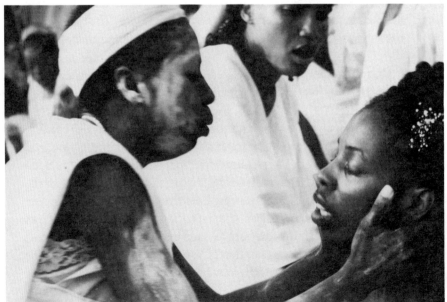

Photo by Sule Greg Wilson

Impressing the Spirit—a priestess imparts insight to the new bride. Ausar Auset group wedding, Prince William Forest Park, Virginia, 1986.

Shinnecock men dancing on their ancestral lands. Many Native American cultures are defined as shamanistic. Annual Labor Day Pow-Pow, Southhampton, New York, 1989.

Priests (males only) in the Western (left-brain dominant) tradition are programmed, culturally, to be less willing to be receptive both to altered states of consciousness and to those who excel at receptivity and the manipulation of emotions, attributes that correspond to the right hemisphere of the brain. Western men aren't "seduced" into receptivity by the sensory overload of music, dance, visualizations, and natural forces (as in possession-trance societies). Their way to separate Spirit from its physical tether is to be assailed physically or deprived sensorially. They "do their thing" alone; you know, the "rugged individualist." There are no priestesses or priest/mediators, no "Mothers of the Gods." The shaman is in the Inner Planes alone. The "trip" is a highly individualized one. And when individuals return from their spiritual voyages their lessons are the mandate of the village. Perhaps it is perceived as more "manly" to feel the Spirit through the decarnating shock of chemicals or physical harrowment than through the soft style of possession, ingesting the rhythm of the music, just letting the Spirit take you. This is what the drum helps you do.

Trance is not difficult; everyone does it every day. Utilizing these natural processes, however, takes awareness and practice. It's really no big thing. Go daydream about it, and get back to me.

6. EMBRACE THE "FEELING" YOU ARE INVOKING

To be a true musician, a master of yourself and your instrument, you must be able instantly to call forth, "visualize" with your hands, for the people before you, whatever energy/deity you are called upon to play. Can you tune your personal energy, drum playing, and chanting to bring to earth a warrior, a military energy, a lover, a mother, a father, enchanter, what have you?

Just as you recognize a blues, a John Philip Sousa march, a Chopin nocturne, or a gospel song from the first notes or chords, so it should also be obvious, from the first note *you* play, just what spiritual power you are invoking, what kind of healing you plan to do. If you have experienced the music before and it is within you, you can play that "feeling," bring forth that emotion, and pass it on to others. Music is about sharing.

When you are familiar with the corresponding elements of a certain power, it is easier to "yoke" the specific energy you are called upon to bring down for the people. Therefore, you must also know the "science of alchemy": use of the appropriate, corresponding colors, scents, images, and dances. Recall your Greek and Roman mythology, read up on the deities of Yoruba and Khamit and the powers and consorts of Buddhism and Hinduism. Read *Longing for Darkness* by China Gallan and the works of J. Olumide Lucas, Godfrey Higgins, and Ra UnNefer Amen. They give alternative views of the "major" religions and alternatives to the religions themselves. They give us the hookups. As the saying goes—there's a future in your past. Mythology is not a "primitive" explanation of the world, it is an allegory of the creation of the psyche of each person.

Joseph Campbell falls short—he chooses stories to illustrate his points, but he doesn't have a universal cosmology into which to fit these tales from around the world. Yes, there is always a Hero, a Great Mother. Does that mean the same thing in each culture? A U.S. "hero" is an unrepentant rogue; a Yoruba one is not. And how does the Hero relate to the King, the Queen, the Jester? Sex has been purged from the West's pantheon; not so in the melanized world. The Supreme Being is universal, yet is descriptively bound by a culture's conceptions and vocabulary. The English word for deity is the same word used for a person who was a de facto slavemaster: "lord." In Khamit and other places in Africa one of God's names is The Great Unknowable, The One Beyond Ken: Amen, Onyame.

A priest carries Ausar, imbibing Oneness, essential Cool. Ausar Auset group wedding, Prince William Forest Park, Virginia, 1986.

African culture is hierarchical; one asks the ancestors to speak to God, like asking your supervisor to speak to the Big Boss, or your congress-woman or -man to speak with the chief executive. And each of these representatives, the deities or saints, have a certain jurisdiction. Their myths describe their bailiwick. The deities exemplify the portions of one's own greater spiritual body. They are the colors hidden in white light. Can you see the rainbow?

Is what you need to play hot and dry Mars/Aries/Heru Khuti/Ogun—with his martial, "kill 'em!" energy—or hot and dry Sun/Heru/Shango, who is solar, regal, loyal, and gregarious? Can you play the difference? Can you *feel* the difference? You must. Are you able to make people feel the party fever of a chant to Aphrodite/Venus/Oshun/Het Heru or the solemnity of Cronos/Saturn/Babaluaye/Sekher's *coro*?

My wife and I were speaking to a couple of women I met in a bead store on Carrol Avenue, in Takoma Park, Maryland. We had them in the living room, explaining how you must be capable of invocation of any power needed, as circumstances demand. I then demonstrated a martial persona, then a venusian one, and then tried to be lunar. It took three tries before I could draw up that cold and moist energy. I had to admit, right there, that Yemoja was not "at my fingertips."

Photo by Sule Greg Wilson

Xiomara Rodriguez demonstrates the Venusian force: Oshun. Orisa Conference, New York City, 1986.

If you don't know the differences between these required energies, you might be bringing forth the correct energy, or you might be just "you" playing "what you feel," an intellectual/emotionally conditioned response that, perhaps, has nothing to do with what is really going on around, within, and through you. No one who's present may consciously know the difference, but you aren't trying to heal them consciously. We're talking Spirit. They'll *feel* the difference, believe me. And however your get-together goes, it goes because of the energy you bring forth. Good times need a musical/spiritual runway to glide in on: a brass bell's tinkle, or a tone so sweet and low.

If you can recall that mellow harmonious feeling then pull it up from your guts, from your "stove"—make it true again right now. I'm sure that everyone has experienced a performance or occasion where, suddenly, everything is flowing, everything is clicking. As the adage says, "The chemistry was there." Indeed it was.

7. RESPECT ANCESTRAL LINES

Each drum family, or orchestra, comes from a certain ancestral line, nation, or "tribe," and, as such, has its own traditional language. Each drum in an orchestra, based on its shape, construction materials, size, and playing technique was developed to speak a particular voice, to sound as its people, to speak to their energy and their forebears. Listen to the *sabarr* drums of the Wolof and listen to the Wolof language. Compare the sound of the *tama* drum in Youssof N'Dour's music to the Yoruba *dun-dun* of King Sunny Adé's. Each hourglass-shaped pressure drum matches in tonal range and playing technique the language the singer is using. It's so, so simple.

That is why so many people from Africa make faces when U.S. drummers perform African music: 'cause what they're saying doesn't make any sense; they're not speaking the language that the drum came from. Sometimes it's as simple as the use of traditional or standard phrasing. Folks who know Western classical or jazz music can tell from the first lick played whether the performers are steeped in that particular tradition or not. One can tell from what they play, from how they stand. It's an outgrowth of the way the acculturated, informed audience lives, how they emote. It's the way they breathe. And if you are outside the tradition, those in the know will judge you by their standard, the tradition you, by using their instruments, are apparently presenting to them.

Ausar Auset drummers, U.S. African representatives to the Jubilee Celebration of the Reinstatement of the Ashanti Confederacy, Kumasi, Ghana, 1985. Pictured are Senemehkhu Enen on cowbell, Sha Serqu Neter on U.S.an kutirinding, and the author on mindroma.

When Vanessa and I went with the Ausar Auset Society to Africa in 1985, and I was asked to take drums, I was keenly aware of that fact. So I made sure I took along drums made in the U.S., with U.S. designs. Since this equipment was *my* territory, and something totally new to the folks in Ghana, no one could question the playing. Some might call that a cheater's way out, I admit, but until we get our own language evolved beyond what we've already developed for the trap set, that's the way to go. Or go Home and study to perfection.

Don't chump U.S. drummers, now; that's not at all what I'm saying. I've heard stories from reliable sources of musicians on the bandstand scheming to affect people's consciousness. For example, I was told that one time a combo conspired to play to make someone take off her clothes; and you know that woman danced right out of her dress. Not a noble use of the technology, but it illustrates a point: Music is power. When you drum, when you make music with people, *you* have power and the issue of control has to be reckoned with. How did *I* learn this? Read on.

Thanksgiving.

How to put on paper what happened between us in the ether? God's blessing of experience, this episode to learn from.

Jody was kind to me, supportive. She was someone to love, to feel attached to, in a cold, small-town Ohio atmosphere of alienation and frustration. I was stuck in a hole I had dug for myself, both personally and academically, and I had to shore up its sides enough to climb out and make my escape to New York City. That took one year. Jody was part of that time—my second and last year at Oberlin College.

Now don't get me wrong—I was there for her, too. A January graduate, she had a degree in French translation and a talent for the flute (and typing). But no plans, no ideas, no specific goals. She took that second semester to gear up for the future back home in Queens, New York.

I'm African American; Jody was Jewish. Our being together didn't sit well with all folks, myself included. But there we were—me estranged and she undecided. I didn't know what was coming, but I was learning to roll with the punches. Though the summer of

'76 back in D.C. had had its good points—seeing old friends, gigging as an African percussionist, playing my mbira, and learning there were some people I really cared about—it had also been a summer of changes. My grandmother's near death over the July 4th weekend and my immersion in family gatherings catalyzed me to my decision: go to New York. That was where the drumming, the culture, the spirituality I needed were to be found. But to get there, I had to transfer schools: so I took the bus back to Ohio early that September.

Though physically at school, I was already gone. I lived off campus—a room in the home of Wendall Logan, Oberlin's jazz professor. I enrolled in jazz orchestra and small ensemble, and even though I got to perform with guest artists such as Abraham Laboriel and Le Roi Jenkins (my street training—real playing—paid off) the music just didn't fit what I heard and felt inside. I was the only percussionist in the orchestra who was playing and not merely reciting. My path to Spirit—New York—was calling.

In big band ensemble is where I met Jody. As the percussionist, I was in the front of the rhythm section, next to and just behind the winds, the flute section. And Jody had first chair. Sexy clothes and classic flautist's posture caught my eye. We struck up a friendship. . . .

Although living with Wendall and family was good—a home away from home, of sorts—just like home there was a rule: no women spending the night. So, most of my time was spent in Jody's white clapboard, off-campus house up on North Michigan, a space she shared with five other Euro-American upperclasswomen and -men; all of them were artistic, literary, saturnine types. I paid them not much mind.

Overall, it was cool. The house had spontaneous poetry readings, Indian print cloth for doors, lots of candles, jazz, and deep conversations. Jody's housemates also rolled with the fact that I, a melanized person, was an intermittent (or was it itinerant?) resident. Scott and Irv were hardly there, Barbara and Margaret were . . . cordial. Megan, who later went to Japan to study traditional paper-making, most often pretended I wasn't there. She ended up impressing me the most, and she was my lesson.

It was Thanksgiving. Back in D.C. my grandmother had recently

*died. I didn't go home, blaming it on midterms. Chico, cajoling
me on the phone, said that my African professors would certainly
be understanding about a death in the family and that I should
come home.*

*I did not go home. In Ohio I was molting, shedding, unraveling old
ways, old views, old fears, old lies. Returning to the bosom of family
would have shattered my fragile, finally independent ego.*

*There was no snow, but there was cold wind. It bit my butt as I
left the institutional vegetarian meal I enjoyed at Afro House. It slid
up my coat and pushed me north, towards the turkey-day party in
honor of Margaret's parents, who had arrived that afternoon from
Cleveland Heights.*

*I helped Jody make some wild rice and after the communally
prepared meal, we—housemates, significant others, and parents—
flopped down onto cast-off furniture and paisley pillows in the
nouveau hippie living room. Parents were there, there was a feeling
of "home" in the air, so we were nice, and warm bellies make warm
smiles. Folks started singing pop songs and clapping along. I went
upstairs to get my brown duffel of percussion instruments I had
schlepped from jazz band rehearsal the day before. Jody assembled
her Armstrong flute, blowing each section to warm it (there's a tonal
difference between a cold instrument and a warm one; just like a
car, just like a drum).*

*After Jody played a couple of tunes—Rampal and Brubeck—I
distributed the percussion instruments, based on my perception of
each person's playing ability. Irv got the agogo (double bell), Barbara
got claves, Margaret and Scott caxixi, the visiting parents got sticks
and maracas, and Megan, Jody, and I played Wendall's box slit
drums.*

*We started with a simple 4/4 rhythm and at first it sounded like
Chicago's "Beginnings." In the spontaneity of the moment everything
came together; we all had fun. But, past the ten-minute mark, lactic
acid built up in folks' forearms and wrists and untrained hands
began to falter. I heard it coming.*

*I took up the slack, directing the energy of the group by increasing
my own intensity (but not volume), playing a harmonizing alto note
that cut across and underneath the other sounds, then slowing the
tempo just enough that everyone could get back on board and lock*

in with the music again. Once the music was secure, I pulled it on up again—just a hair—to give each of the players some renewed exhilaration.

The music stood up proud! I breathed easy and listened, just playing along. But then . . . a nudge, a discord came. Someone was fighting—seriously, consciously fighting—what I was doing! With ears and energy perked I tuned from player to player: Irv was solid on bell: "DAM-DAM, Dee! DAM-DAM, d'Dee! DAM-DAM, Dee! DAM-DAM, d'Dee!" Okay! Claves are on the one, the caxixi were xixi-ing in time, Jody's rhythm was holding up, the parents on maracas and sticks are fine, so who . . . ?

Megan! Her new one-two, one-two, one-two beat was changing up the groove, diverting the tempo, hurrying and harrying the music. Ahhh . . .

I didn't turn; no need to. She and I were ninety degrees from each other, how did we wind up sitting nearly back to back? The others, slumped forward in concentration or with heads thrown back, eyes closed, were to my left and before me. I heard in myself, "let's see what happens."

I brought up the intensity, just a little. There she was! Pushing, prodding, jerking like a fish on a baited hook, nibbling for control. I gave her some slack, retracting my energy from the ensemble, letting hers get past to influence the whole.

For two heartbeats it shimmied, then began to follow her lead: "A-dung-doonk! A-dung-doonk! A-dung-doonk! A-dung-doonk! A-dung-doonk!" For a moment, I felt—this just may work.

Not. After about fifteen measures the music began to slide, to waver in its tracks like a new-walking toddler. . . . It shook, staggered and almost fell.

I came back up. Again Megan fought, clenching for control. But it had already crested. Here was a chance to harmonize. The music continued.

I don't think anyone else noticed what transpired that evening. No one spoke a word to me about it while we were playing or later when folks took their leave. Megan had talked to me through music, telling me how she felt and what she wanted to do and control, just as in a letter or a telephone call. I heard what she had to say.

That incident demonstrated for me that I wanted control and order in the music I was part of, and that I could have it, could take it, could make use of it. I also saw that I was willing to not fight and to let someone else take over. But when the harmony fell, I assserted control and form to maintain the music for everyone. Learning consciously to do that was a godsent message and gift.

Thanks, Megan. Happy Thanksgiving.

8. KNOW YOUR ORCHESTRATION

There are three basic voices to African and Diaspora drums: mother, father, and child (or bass, treble, and midrange). In some societies it is the mother, in others it's the father that is the heavy-pitched, authority-talking drum. From my experience, the child is always high- to midrange, and keeps a steady rhythm. Think of a talkative four-year-old. Now take a minute to think of music you know; you'll see that the instrumentation of drum ensembles has developed to encompass these three basic families of sound.

In the West, people are trained to appreciate the high end of the musical spectrum: the tenor and soprano voices. This "ear training" carries over to one's expectation of how a drum orchestra should be constructed. Therefore take note: even though the "lead"or "solo" drum is high-pitched, (the *quinto* of the conga drum ensemble, or the lead djembe), the real talker/invoker, the one that sets the pace, is often the low-pitched, bottom drum: *iya* in the *bata* orchestra, *jun-jun* in the djembe orchestra, or a conga *tumbao*. Listen to *The Drummer's Path* audiocassette/CD of the conga, djembe, and *jun-jun* orchestras. This correlates with the effect that chanting high or low has on a person's own spirit. High notes excite, but low ones entrance. Think of the feeling you get when you hear opera diva Kathleen Battle, then Paul Robeson's "Ole Man River." Or James Earl Jones as the voice of Darth Vader. Or how a good subwoofer attacks your guts. Low tones have an almost overt physical effect.

How does one learn these parts, if the music isn't written? Use your body as the scribe, the stylus, and papyrus. Thus: whenever you play with an orchestra or listen to one, investigate; take the time to attend to the parts interlocking. Find the bass, the bottom part, be it *jun-jun*, *bolon*, or bass fiddle, then walk up the combo from there. Feel where in your body each rhythm hits, and cement that picture right there, never to leave.

It's the same with U.S. Dixieland music, another musical form that flows and shares. Go inside and dissect the music, use your ear to go from one part to the other, from banjo to piano, from clarinet to trumpet, and absorb how each person's contribution relates to what the other musicians are playing. Once this is studied, you will have all the parts, and their proper execution, at your disposal.

You had better. Because one day, almost certainly, you will be called upon to teach others music. Or circumstances may demand you to carry the weight, or even play alone. If that happens, you'll have to play solo as if all those other parts were there to lend you their support. They'll be there, too—if you can retrieve the sound of the other instruments from their store-spots in your body, and play that back and listen to them in your head as you present. Having that full sound, if only in your head, will help your execution.

Let me share with you a story about the power of orchestration.

The Bata ensemble. The deep-toned iya *("mother" in the Yoruba language) is the center, lead drum. Orisa Conference, New York City, 1986.*

Photo by Sule Greg Wilson

The Shango drum orchestra of Trinidad and Tobago. Orisa Conference, New York City, 1986.

African ensembles are not just drums: Dagomba musicians from north-ern Ghana play the zaabia rattle and gondze one-string fiddle. Smithsonian Institution's Festival of American Folklife, Washington, D.C., 1976.

I could tell fall was coming. The Sunday afternoon air in New York's Central Park was turning golden, but golden in a thin, brittle light that reminded me of frosty breath, dry hands, and apple juice boiled over by mistake. Juice! Give me liquid! I needed a drink right now, right then. I yearned for a cold, sugary quart of apple juice that could pare this Big City dust and grit from my hoarse and swollen throat. I sing in my throat when I'm playing hard.

And after nearly six hours of street-jam playing, it was hard. Folks—good drummers—had come, sat in, and gone. Now, late in the day, it was only the stragglers, those folks desperate as I to quench whatever inner thirst they slaked by hanging out all day, floating from jam session to drummer's circle to the end.

My canvas drum bag, folded under my rump for protection against those open-slat wooden park benches, was getting seriously humidified, and my ears rang from cowbells and broomsticks and Heineken bottles and concrete chunks and sticks being beaten on the back of the bench and beer cans shaken with pebbles inside. . . .

The curly-haired Latino on my right playing the tumbao *kept smiling at me. His dark eyes twinkled, and he kept pumping away and smiling and playing the wrong parts for the kind of drum he had between his legs. It was getting hard to smile back. He was doing a middle (conga) part on a low-sound bottom drum, which forced me to counterbalance with a bottom part played on my higher drum that had to be played harder—to be heard and felt—and I was killing myself.*

The other drummer, the one on my left, didn't know much more. He was riffing, and his pops and his rolls and his slaps and his tones were . . . well, now, I really don't know. Was he really good and playing in and around the clave—and throwing the bell player off—or was he bad—and the bell player was trying to get him back on track? Whatever the reason, I knew I'd be peeing blood tonight. And the sun was going down.

We were losing it, I could tell. The people standing around us were getting vacant expressions, and not because we were entranc-ing them with sound. Perhaps we were deadening them. I was getting depressed.

Then that golden evening light highlit a face in the crowd, a teak-

brown face framed in dredlocks and spherical specs. Hey! I knew that face!

Though I didn't know her by name, this wiry, wide-hipped Sister and I had exchanged respectful glances at many cultural events in the City. I had seen her play at bembes *and on stage, wielding her* sekere *as only a master can. Which, as she stepped to the inside of the circle, she proceeded to do.*

I smiled at her; gratefully, I'm sure. She nodded in return, and unpacked her axe. She swung:

Cha-CHOONG! Ta-ta-te; Ta, ta, ta! Cha-CHOONG! Ta-ta-te; Ta, ta, ta! Cha-CHOONG! Ta-ta-te; Ta, ta, ta! Cha-CHOONG! Ta-ta-te; Ta, ta, ta! Cha-CHOONG! . . .

Music to my ears! My toes curled in my sneakers! I was back in the game again! And playing with no fatigue. She played the rhythm that brought us all together, that unified the different levels of interest, expectation, and expertise that the other musicians were expressing. She made us whole. And we sounded good, too.

Photo by Masashi Ohtsu

Gourd music in concert: Women of the Calabash. Left to right: Madeline Yayodele Nelson, Joan Ashley, Natalie Ransom.

See, y'all, when you make this music, all of the parts must be at your beck and call, locked within your spirit and ready to fly. If you're stuck in a situation similar to the one I just recounted, you'll know what to play to bring it all together, as Yayodele did.

This knowledge is appropriate for any situation. To compensate for or complement a new dancer you may have to play a different accompaniment part than the one you first learned. Or one day you'll have to play lead, or incorporate middle, bass, and top parts into one rhythm. Of course, you've got to know the rhythms to use them. And if your visualization is good, your music will sound, or at least feel, as if a full orchestra were right there playing.

For optimum transmission of the drummer's spiritual energy to the congregation there must be harmonious and sufficient density of sound. A full spectrum, from low rumbles to high tinkles, carries the energy projected by the musicians and overloads the senses of each listener. And if the musicians are all "in tune" with the invocation energy, the dancers are all "overloaded" with the same energy, or thought-forms. Then trance comes faster, the ritual is over sooner, and the drummers don't have to play so long. Amen.

9. INTERNAL, EXTERNAL, AND PERIPHERAL AWARENESS

As you watch people dance, focus on them and their movements. The movements are reflections of the forces coming to them and through them. Observe, and absorb the rhythms their bodies are making. It is "the gods" talking. Listen with your eyes.

When you observe, you can intuit and ingest energy from the dancers and know which of their motions needs to be accented. Then you can give the energy right back to them. In his book *The Healing Drum*, Yaya Diallo speaks of recognizing disharmonies in people's spirits by observing their dancing. He, or his teachers, would then switch the rhythm around to help the person out. I wish everyone knew this. There's almost nothing more painful for a dancer than to be beat down with the music when it's supposed to be taking them up higher. Proficiency at this comes with time, practice, going within, "feeling out" what you need and how you need to be playing. Intuition wedded with the technique to play exactly what you see someone doing grows into the ability to play what the person needs to hear and feel. Doing this and not losing your

Walter Ince and Olukose Wiles intuit each other's music to perform pinpoint-accurate percussion.
Akanni *(drum call), Flushing Meadow Park, New York, 1977.*

place in the ongoing music is what you're aiming for. Remember: the best solo/lead is one that meshes, is a part of the music that pulls all the musicians to a point of focus on the dancer.

Lead parts are just that: parts. Often what the lead drummer plays could, when played with the intensity focused in toward the ensemble, be accompaniment parts. What the lead part says relates directly to what the dancers, drummers, and chanters are doing and feeling. Even sparsely played notes are executed only within the context of the density of sound created within the interlocking parts played by the orchestra as a whole. The bass, bell, and chanting are like the bass line and chords of Western music: you must follow it, harmonize with it in your lead parts. You can't leave the clave. If you do, you're speaking English when everyone else is speaking Spanish.

This awareness also carries into other aspects of your life. Suddenly you're seeing new things, or old things in new ways. Check it out.

When I arrived at Oberlin College in September 1975, there were three conga men already on the scene: Kerry, an African-American from Baltimore; Bobby, a Puerto Rican—from New York, I think— and Adam, a Euro-American.

Unpacking my bags in my new dorm room in Dascomb Hall, I didn't know what to expect. Someone had told me there were African percussionists about. But where? How would I meet them? How good would they be? What could I learn? And who was gonna be my roommate? What about classes and girls? And how was I gonna find room for my two congas, clothes, books, records, and record player in this little room?

I had the door to room 144 swung wide, letting in air, helping me feel not so constricted in that two-bed, ten-foot-square room. I turned toward the mirror hung between the matched oak closets, wondering where to put my socks, when someone ran by. I started when he popped his head back in.

He was white, and medieval-looking, with the long face, spare moustache, goatee, and military helm haircut you associate with Gothic walls and illuminated manuscripts. He stepped into the room, stuck out an amazingly small hand, and introduced himself.

"Hi. I hear you're new. I'm Adam."

Adam! One of the drummers! Who, as I found out in the next few minutes, had gone to New York last January and studied with the legendary Ladji Camara of Guinea for his winter term project. Adam was familiar with the legendary djembe drum, and he studied percussion in the Conservatory. He had come to Dascomb Hall to find out about the new drummer in town. He even beat my room-mate to the place.

Right then and there, in town only a few hours, with no friends or acquaintances, I began to draw back from Adam. Not because he was white; that was no problem. Kevin, another Euro-American, was my conga practice partner for a while in high school. We had both been dissed by the same Dominican "master drummer," so we found solace in Mongo records and each other's company.

My problem with Adam wasn't race, it was culture. A culture that, up until that very moment, I had not known I possessed. It was nothing conscious, just something absorbed. In my studies to that point I had occasionally been in the drummers' circle, trying to hang, but mainly I stood without that circle, watching and quietly learning. Watching men (and sometimes women) enter that circle and seeing how they did it. Watching them leave—and how and when they did it. Who spoke, and when, and to whom.

And as I quietly unpacked my clothes at Oberlin College, wonder-ing how to hook up with the drummers of the school, I was acting in tune with that culture.

Adam was without. How? Why? What rules did he break? Just one. A simple one: know your place.

I was the newcomer, the untried one. The one who had to prove his worth. I had to be the one to stand outside the circle, demon-strating with body language, concentration, attention, relaxation, harmonizing "vibes," and radiated power that I could hang, that my playing would not disrupt the circle; that I would fit.

Adam, running over to find the new drummer in town, showed me he wasn't acculturated to the protocols of the drum. Therefore, he was potentially dangerous. His act was out of harmony. It demonstrated a yearning beyond discipline, beyond propriety. Dangerous.

Nevertheless, we played. He showed me what he had learned, and I shared what I could. But his heart had come from somewhere else than mine.

Needless to say, at Oberlin, a college that prided itself on its classical music tradition and its Conservatory, there was, among the general population, a smug disaffection toward African drumming. It manifested in different ways. The Oberlin Review *ran a photograph of me, Bobby, and an unidentified Euro-American playing outside Dascomb Hall. The caption described us as playing "the simple, rhythmic conga" drums. I never did write that "letter to the editor," though I've composed it in my head a million times.*

Between the north and south campuses at Oberlin, is a cement tunnel about forty yards long. It was a tradition, I found, for Oberlin drummers to play there, letting the concrete walls magnify the sound of the conga drums.

One still-cool evening, the spring after my arrival at Oberlin, Adam and I were playing in the tunnel. Hunched together and getting down, we were generally oblivious to any passersby. But one, a white male in jeans and a tie-dyed T-shirt, caught our attention. He tossed a penny at our feet, never losing stride, never looking back.

Adam understood, as did I, the intent of that gesture. The coin came at us as change to an organ grinder's monkey. I stared after his back but Adam, suddenly red in the face, jumped up, snatched up the penny, and threw it at the young walker's head. He cupped his hands and yelled after him, "We don't play for money!" The penny didn't hit the guy. And he never turned around.

Did you ever hear anyone say "don't touch my drum" or "don't lean on it"? In some societies, customs have developed to protect the invokers of Spirit and their instruments. The Yoruba tradition in the New and the Old World forbids the handling of certain drums, such as the *bata,* unless you have been spiritually prepared and ritually cleansed. Custom dictates that one should never touch India's tabla-bayan drums with one's came-in-contact-with-all-kinds-of-soils feet. In the Asante tradition, the Asantehene (king) has drums which are played only by the most revered and eldest musicians. This respect for localized spiritual power is almost universal. In Marion Zimmer Bradley's Arthurian romance *The Mists of Avalon,* the tradition is that no one may take, borrow, or touch the harps of the Jali, or Bard. I have learned the "why" of that tradition. I learned it up in Harlem.

I left Oberlin in June 1977 and moved to New York City to continue my drumming and spiritual studies and to get a college degree I could live with. I transfered to New York University to study TV production. My cousin Sandy, who was on scholarship at Alvin Ailey's, let me crash at her place in Manhatton that first summer in New York.

The apartment, a four-flight roach-infested two-and-a-half-room walk-up on the East Side, facing the Queensboro Bridge, was a five-minute walk from the old Ailey East Side studio. In 1977 the neighborhood was not good news. But beggars can't be choosers.

From Sandy's apartment on 59th Street, I trekked around the City to play and learned how far I still had to go toward the intensity of energy needed to really do the music the way it should be done. Through Steve Berrios (Mongo's drummer) and his New York connections I found exactly what I needed, what I had come to New York to find: a dance and drum class run by folks who knew the folklore of what they were doing (see the Afterword). These people had the right drums, the right songs, the right dances, even the right clothes. It was all there. It was heaven, way out in St. Albans, Queens.

But things change. Sandy gave up her dance classes at Ailey's and her apartment and New York City, and that meant I had to move. And had to change. The classes in St. Albans were energizing me, galvanizing me, crystallizing my purpose. Invited to hang out with International's (IAAB) drummers on the weekends, I participated in ceremonies that demanded hours of playing and weeks of study. The Gods came down. I saw percussion in practical use, part of a way of life. It sank in. My road was clear.

Home to Harlem

*Somehow, Jody knew
When I left that night—I was never
Coming back.*

*She ran after me.
Walking to the bus stop, ten p.m.
Suddenly there she was behind me,
and so apologetic.*

She said she was sorry,
Whatever she might have said,
Whatever it could have been.

Sorry for what?
For being just what she was?

That Summertime, nighttime crossroads was hot, and humid.

But not the
Humidity of People,
Of Harlem, where I had just moved.

It was the humidity of trees,
and ease,
and White Folks living

and land with less than a generation of
Coverage by the city.
Fumes of ignorant luxury oozing up around my ankles.

Leaving her at the crossroads
I had turned
From College towns, and country
Air; from Childhood's reckless acts;
And folks who'd love
To be of your Becoming—

Yet offer
Nothing

But to hold
You back.

Where I went was Uptown, to Harlem, to my uncle Hugh's apart-
ment on the famous Sugar Hill. While living there I learned my
lesson about the sanctity of one's instrument. Remember The Mists
of Avalon?

I moved into my cousin Hugh Junior's room, overlooking the Alexander Hamilton residence—the Grange—at 141st Street and Convent Avenue. It was fair, 'cause at the exact same time Hugh Junior was living with my parents, back in my bedroom, in D.C. But it was a chore. All my equipment—books upon books, albums upon albums, record player, clothes, two conga drums, drum seat, and drum stands—was compressed into one room of a two-bedroom apartment. Hugh Junior's stuff was still there, too: baseball trophies, records, bed, dresser, desk, table, bench. I know Uncle Hugh and Aunt Sylvia had to shake their heads when I came in. But bless them, they let me be and let me stay with them for nine months until I moved to that one-room in Bed-Stuy, Brooklyn, owned and managed by my drum teacher Olukose's mother and aunt.

The lesson came thus: Hugh's place had been my home now for just a month. I was glad to be living with family. It gave me a chance to get acclimated to New York City: to NYU, to the subways, to the hustle and bustle and the opportunities that the Big City offered. Those first weeks in September I was never home. I hung out with Tommy Graham, the percussionist who lived one floor below me in the nine-story building. He toured me, going up the street to Jesse Oliver's classes at City College ("I want a Funga!" Jesse would shout, brandishing his fine oak chalkboard pointer, and the cast of thousands of drummers would all look at each other in confusion); to Olukose's classes in Queens; to Central Park on Sundays to jam; or downtown to the Village. I learned the drummer's city.

And I discovered how high my expectations of excellence were. I came to see that the drive that compelled me, the steep angle of the Path I was treading, would consummate at a place far beyond where some other folks had settled. Tommy was the vehicle for this. One Wednesday night he came calling, and we strolled over to Malcom X Boulevard to watch the resident African Dance Company at rehearsals and tryouts. The ground-floor gym/studio was wall-to-wall niggas—as the saying goes in Harlem, in August. Dancing. Talk about hot! But, hey, people just took it in stride, so I did too.

I watched a light-skinned Sister—pretty brown bush and big brown eyes—take the congregated hopefuls across the floor with some fancy Mali dance combinations. After the "go!" drum break was played, people flailed across the floor, turning talk with the body into babble with the limbs. And the drum sounds boomed off hardwood floors to ricochet away from the cinder-block walls. The vibes were catching; the drums pulsed. I felt my heartbeat quicken, my posture get better, and my breathing grow shallower. I wanted to play.

The musicians: bulky conga players, a huge sekere man, small, dark djembe-ites, and songba players of yellow and brown, were lined up against one wall. The not-tall brother in charge of the drumming, a wiry, black-coffee-colored man with just the beginning of dreds, saw me chafing at the bit to put my two cent's worth of energy in. After walking inspection down the line one more time he went to a bag on the bleachers and handed me a cowbell and a simple part to play. He placed me with the bell section and let me go. Given that taste of creative freedom, I let the bell sing until the cows came home.

And when that evening's class was over I kept my ringing ears open and learned that some of those flailing folks who seemed—to me—beginning dancers were the featured performers of the company. Oh. I see. Each one seeks their own level. Keeping my options open, I thanked the leaders and moved on.

One day, one cloudy not yet biting cold November Saturday afternoon, Tommy came trekking upstairs to 5-B, with a vaguely familiar friend in tow. I answered the door—Aunt Sylvia was checking store coupons and Uncle Hugh was constructing another bookcase—and led the two through the narrow, book-lined hallway to my room in the back.

I gestured them toward the two-seater balister-backed bench under the window. I took the single bed opposite. Lanky, café-au-lait Tommy folded himself and his ever-present Army-surplus jacket onto the bench. He introduced Kenny: "He's a drummer, too; lives over in East Harlem. Used to play with Ladji [Ladji Camara of Guinea, grandfather of djembe playing in America]."

Kenny was younger, smaller, browner than Tommy, and with the brittled eyes and dark-stained fingertips you only catch glimpses of on vid bites on the local evening news. Or the subway. If you're lucky. Kenny didn't flop, he just sat down and slid back into the chair.

"So, man, what's up?" Tommy's bony fingers crossed and uncrossed, stroked the knit multicolored kufi on his head. "Wha'cha doin' today?"

I looked from one guest to the other, then laid back on the bed's foam cushion. "Nothin'. I really don't know. Not yet."

"Okay," Tommy looked at Kenny, "'cause Kenny's got a gig today— a bembe *up in the Bronx—and he rehearses in Brooklyn, so all his stuff's down there. . . ."*

*I looked past their left shoulders to my drums in the corner behind the clothes rack: two maple-stained Gon Bops congas that I'd paid for with summer job money and refinished myself—*quinto *and* segundo *that I'd bought from Drums Unlimited in Bethesda, Maryland, just the year before . . . my drums, that I carried on my back all the way here from D.C. and Ohio and back and forth from Olatunji's on 125th Street to 141st Street in the snow in January. . . .*

In that silence Tommy sat and looked sincere; Kenny, kinda sheepish for leaving his axe in another borough. "We figured since you've got two. . . ."

There it was—the vise. I was pressured on two fronts. I've got to be a Brother to a Brother drummer in need, trying to make a living, and I can't show myself as a selfish son of a bitch who won't let even·one of his drums out of his sight.

I sat up and let out a deep breath. The two of them sank deeper into their chairs. With my gaze I let Tommy know this was happen-ing only because he was the one came up and asked. He got the message. They both smiled.

As I closed the metal-sheathed door of the apartment behind them, I thought "Who is this guy?" I had been hanging out and playing with the drummers from International. I knew how hard they worked at bembes *and how much technical expertise and spiritual power they had to squeeze out of themselves at every "Ago!" and downbeat. Kenny did not look to be in their league. I did not have a good feeling about that loan.*

Late that evening Tommy dropped off my drum. I felt like a parent waiting up, listening for familiar footsteps. At the door, he passed the conga inside with an apology about having to get to bed . . . "Forget it, Tommy." I shut, locked, and checked the door. I sighed. Everything seemed all right as I shouldered the drum and carried it into the back. I unpacked it immediately. It wasn't broken, or scarred—Lord knows, I checked for that immediately. There was no physical damage at all. I tapped it, rubbed it, smelled it. Nothing I could see, but something was just not right. I remembered Olukose's admonition after one bembe, *as we wiped the sweat, and packed up instruments, and ate delicious food: "Take a piece of fruit with you as you leave the ceremony. Go to the crossroads and wipe yourself down with it, then throw it over your shoulder into the street." He explained further that people go to these services to be released; sometimes what comes off of them jumps onto you. Scrape them vibes off onto the banana, let it fly, and then walk on. I did as he said and never forgot.*

Handling my drum after it came back from Kenny's gig in the Bronx gave me a static charge, tangible as the push-back you feel when trying to force two like-pole magnets together, aware in your fingers of that slimy counterpressure. The drum radiated strangeness, as when you're standing right next to someone who's just had a terrible, terrible shock. What could I do then?

This was my drum, come back to me. I was happy—it was back, and intact. But the vibes, they had me worried. I didn't know to what kind of place my conga went, or what for. Or the spiritual state of whomever had touched it, had played it, energized it. What had it been through, absorbed?

Though I Florida-Watered it and rubbed it down, it took a long while, a good long while before I could sense my drum was once again clean. What I had intellectually "known" before, about vibes and other folks, I had now lived. And my drums, from then on, went only with me. Anywhere.

10. LEARN THE TECHNIQUE SPECIFIC TO YOUR DRUM

Each drum demands the development of a different set of muscles and calluses. *Shiko* is not conga is not djembe. Nor is a *donno* a *dun-dun* or a *tama.*

You can sometimes tell what kind of instrument a person plays by the muscles they've developed and, definitely, by the calluses on their hands. Conga requires much upper body strength—chest and biceps—while djembe is empowered through the back. Djembe's energy flow comes through the underside of your arms, through elbow and wrist to hand—more yin—while the conga demands so much energy flowing through your pectoral muscles. It's amazing. But then djembe was designed to be a healing drum, so of course it would work through the nurturing yin.

To play the drum correctly you *must* be relaxed. Conga came from a different climatic (forest, not savannah) and ritual (multiethnic) tradition. And techniques don't trade both ways. Here is my experience of learning that:

I mean, I knew I could play conga, and Adam had showed me the slaps he had learned at Ladji Camara's studio. So back home in D.C., the summer of '76, I was—I thought—prepared when I sat behind a djembe at Baile's studio on 14th Street and Park Road. As the elder carved out a drum shell, I tried my usual conga cup-hand slap on this other goatskin-headed drum. I expected a resonant K-annng! *Instead I got something like this:* PFFT. *It takes a while to learn to relax the right way to play the powerful djembe drum.*

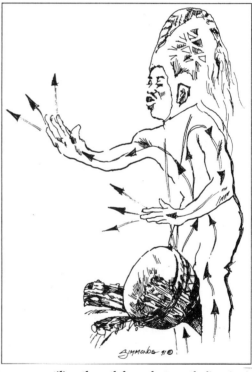

Illustrations by Oswald Simmonds, Jr.

The flow of energy through drummers. The congero utilizes the path from sky to earth, directing it through the extensor muscles of the outer arms and through the external obliques, the pectoral muscles, quads, gastrocnemius, and out. The djembe player directs energy up, ultimately coming through the rhomboidius, trapezius, flexors, and out. Use of different sets of muscles demands different paths of energy. Try it; find it.

Each drum, or each drum family, requires specialized training, just the way violin or viola, cello or bass, piccolo or B-flat flute do. Don't chump yourself or the instrument, saying, "I play one, I can play them all." With a strong foundation in one instrument, you can apply the techniques and principles to assist in learning other instruments. That's part of the reason for this book. But you can't just pick 'em up. There is different embouchure for trombone and for trumpet. There is different technique for *jun-jun* and tamboura. Remember the saying: "A jack of all *tabl* and master of none. . . ."

Illustration by Oswald Simmonds, Jr., from a photograph in *Drums in the Americas.*

Euro-Americans outlawed hand drums, so disguiseable alternative drum shells were used: barrels, mortars, buckets. Shown here are typical U.S. African percussion instruments; their popular use has dwindled with urbanization and access to machine-made and Western instruments and culture. Right to left, counterclockwise: triangle, Bel Tambouye drum, banjo, sheep shanks, Tom-Tom, harmonica, a large Ka drum (the U.S. version of conga), gourd rattle tied to a staff, quills, wood flute, bones, jaw bone, comb, Jew's harp. The comb (and tissue) is a folk kazoo.

I've spoken with other drummers about this, and they concur—you can go from playing conga to djembe, but it doesn't work the other way around quite so easily. It is of course possible, but what you learn on djembe doesn't cross, doesn't translate, to the slat-made, cow- or mule-skin-headed conga drum. How one uses one's hands to sound that thick skin is totally different from the technique for a thin goat- or calfskin, which you find on djembe. The wrist control and strength one gains from conga *can* prepare one for the lightness, timing, sounding technique, and phrasing of the djembe.

Djembe is in fashion today. Conga drums have been popular in the United States for more than forty years (it's part of the Motown sound), and the drum's science is closer to those hand drums that survived here on the mainland up into the twentieth century. (See the illustration on page 74.) Also, conga is a synthetic drum culture, descended from the merger in Cuba of many traditions of West and Central Africa. This harmonizes with the mixed ancestry of most of the inhabitants of these western Atlantic shores. The conga, as a closer ancestor, can perhaps lead the way to drum families further back in one's percussion family tree. Listen to your heart. Listen to "Opening of the Way," "Djembe Lamba," and "Baya" on *The Drummer's Path* audiocassette/CD, in which the djembe and conga traditions are brought together. Compare the voicing, the invocations that each drum makes. Realize that each one takes work. Then do it.

11. KNOW STICK TECHNIQUE

Here in the West, when someone mentions stick technique, the image that flashes forth is snare drum or trap set. Sure, any rudiments are useful, but African drums demand a different kind of stroke. The cycles and mechanics of rhythm, the choice of materials for shell and skin and stick, the aesthetics all work to determine the sound you get. It can be a tricky business.

When playing with sticks, be careful not to play linearly (see illustration on page 77). Each stroke you put to the drum or bell must be part of a cycle that returns the energy that you put out back into your person and into the people before you. If you play *down* into the instrument, all you are doing is breaking it to pieces, dissipating your energy, and disappointing those whose chakras wait to catch your sent emotions. Play the "Solo for Songba" on *The Drummer's Path* audiocassette/CD. Can you hear the drum stroke reverberating off the back head of the drum? And the open and closed tones on the playing head?

When playing stick on skin, play "away" from the drum head. The intent of the musician is invocation of the spirit/voice of the instrument, not to beat it until it screams. Focus your energy so that it flows the length of the stick and whips away, like snapping a towel or skipping a stone on water; gentle as touching a child to wake her. Focus your energy to that one point you strike on the drum's surface, not beyond it. Transfer your energy into the instrument—firmly, yet gently—stroking it until it purrs and converses, that's what we want.

When playing a two-headed instrument, you must feel the energy you release move from the head you struck to the opposite head, sound upon it, and bounce back again. You should feel an echo, a rebound of sound within the drum's shell. That way the energy circulates, comes back, and you can use it again. On *The Drummer's Path* audiocassette/ CD you can hear the energy coming back when I'm playing my newly developed Usonium drums. When the head is struck, the sound reverberates from the skin head to the drum's metal bottom and back, then

Compare these Algerian street musicians to the U.S. street musician depicted in the "Camptown Races" sheet music illustration (page 23); notice the similar stick technique in this 19th-century engraving. Both have transverse drums, curved sticks, and left hand free. Notice the drummer's relaxation; he could play all day.

Illustration by Oswald Simmonds, Jr.

What you see here—in exaggerated form—will save you from re-placing drum heads, and the use of arnica for pain (see "Health and the Drummer"). From above and below, energy is directed from the Kundu, down the arm, along the length of the stick, which then strokes—only strokes—the drum head. Energy is transferred through the drumhead to the other head, back and out. When the drumshell rings, you've got control.

out the hole in the bottom. If you don't feel that slight kickback in your hands and vibration throughout the body of the drum (you can hear the metal cans sending out overtones on the recording), you're not playing correctly. The whole drum has to sing.

The technology of "throwing energy" applies to playing any drum, to dancing, or to any martial art. Send your energy out so that it can return. If you throw it away, you can hurt yourself and you get tired almost immediately. It's like pacing yourself when you're jogging or sparring. You learn just how much energy to put out to get the desired result and how much to retain so you don't falter.

And what's with all this tape on sticks and hands? Drumming is about skin on skin, life force being transmitted; adhesive tape or duct tape short-circuit you, and only make it worse in the long run. The glue

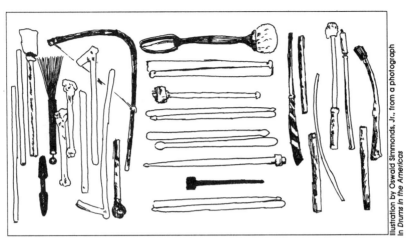

Illustration by Oswald Simmonds, Jr., from a photograph in *Drums in the Americas*

Get the right tool for the job. Drumsticks—African, Native, and Euro-American.

sticks to your hand and tears it up. Then you get blisters. Or blood.

Yes, if you don't do this you'll get calluses. But dead skin is cheaper than buying and depending on plastic and glue. And calluses are a great gauge of how proficient at technique you are. At first you'll bleed, then you get lots of protective skin; eventually (if you continue to hone your technique) the protective callus shrinks to just what you need to slide that stick into place on the drumhead. No lumpy bumps confessing that you've still got to vise the stick to keep it from flying away. Be gentle, but firm. Eventually, with technique and care, the calluses lessen. It's amazing.

One more thing: don't forget to use the appropriate sticks. I've had more than one bell and drum broken by someone using a stick with too much weight behind it. Research the instrument: is it supposed to be played with a short, curved stick; a long, padded one; a rubber-tipped one; a long, curved one; a bald one? If you don't have the right stick, you don't get the right sound. You wouldn't use a cello bow to play a violin, would you?

12. ORCHESTRATE OTHER PERCUSSION INSTRUMENTS

My experience has been that most people consider bells and shakers to be just "miscellaneous percussion," things to have around to play so you can participate and not be in the way. There is an element of truth to that; that context does exist. But in this realm, we know better.

There is a proper way to hold the bell and its stick. A bell *is* an instrument and must be held to release its optimum level of vibration, just as a piano's strings are dampened or not, at the discretion of the musician. How many good instruments have been lost from people beating them down? Let's envision a typical LP-type cowbell, for example. If you beat the lip of one of those bells, you're just banging it to pieces. Just behind the edge, or three-quarters of the bell's distance from lip to base, are good sound points. So is the curve where the seam weld is. A Guinea bell—a *bala*—is hand-forged from iron. Play it wrong and it just tinkles to shreds.

Search for the instrument's voice; give it, and yourself, time. Good playing is making the dancers feel the music of the orchestra, not having them cringe because *you* want to be heard. Listen to your bell's part and the other parts' interrelation: are you complementing, or are you just doubling a part someone else is already speaking through?

There are whole orchestras of just bells and gongs out there in the world. Listen to "Iron and Steel" on *The Drummer's Path* audiocassette/CD for samples of bell orchestration. If you want to go far afield, check out Indonesia's gamelan tradition. Led by drums, the gamelan

Photo by Sule Greg Wilson

Kendang agung—*"the leader of time, large size"*—*the two-headed lead drum of the gamelan orchestra. To the drummer's right is the* kendang ciblon *(midsized drum) and, in the background, are* bonang *pot gongs.*

There you have it: dance, drums, song, Spirit. Earth and sky—harmonized. Agogo, Ghana, 1985

also includes brass gongs, xylophones, and bells and is a joyous sound to hear. All of the principles found here also apply to that Indonesian percussion orchestra. The funkiest gamelan music is found in Bali, the southern part of that nation of islands. In India, one must also go south to find the "down-home" sounds. *Mridangam* is the *bata* of India.

Sekere orchestras also break down into "family" sounds, as drums and handclaps do. Before playing one, realize this: *sekere* is really two instruments played simultaneously: the gourd itself and the surrounding net. Before you go *shika-shika-shika*, practice with the calabash alone; get to know it, master it. Get a good *POP!* and *GOONG!* from the base and *SMACK!* from the neck before you tackle the net. Gourds with and without nets are featured in "Calabash" on *The Drummer's Path* audiocassette/CD. Get to know these sounds on your instrument. Then make it talk for you and for the world, seen and not-seen.

That's it. You ask, will using these Principles make you a better drummer? No, not in and of themselves. You and the Spirit with you will have to see to that. The Principles are only tools, reminders, and guidelines to simplify and harmonize the art of making music, of sharing your energy with the world around you. That's all.

FOUR

HEALTH AND THE DRUMMER

There are certain problems that will attack any musician: tendinitis, eyestrain, fatigue. There are some that drummers alone must cope with.

Drummers' bodies undergo great internal stress, as well as the trauma to palms, arms, and shoulders from the shock of contact with skin or wood. Some drummers sing or speak when they play, putting pressure on vocal chords and cranial blood vessels. Some elicit needed energy from their bodies by tightening stomach and torso muscles, squeezing their viscera and putting undue strain on internal organs. These harsh practices do release energy, but at a high cost. There are other, less destructive, more efficient ways.

Through controlling the breath, the perineum, the urinary and anal sphincters—as described in Mantak Chia's books (see Bibliography) and in *Taoist Yoga* by Lu K'uan Yu—by maintaining correct posture and by staying relaxed, one can tap reserves of primal/natal energy without overtaxing the body or putting it through unnecessary stress.

Techniques such as these were taught to me as part of my priesthood training in the Ausar Auset Society. I have practiced them and seen them work. They have helped make me a better person and musician.

My musicianship and spiritual acumen have grown hand in hand. I started drumming and dancing in junior high school, and around that same time is when I began to think about my diet. Eventually I became a vegetarian. You say you "have to" have your meat? You may be right—for you—but hear me out.

Generally speaking, your eating habits help determine how your spiritual growth is going to go. If your body isn't clean, your perceptions of the world around you, seen and unseen, are going to be distorted. Having a junk-fooded-up body and trying to perceive the subtler realms of Spirit is just like trying to examine an engraving through warped or dirty glass. You don't get exactly the right picture. You may think you see a monster, but all that horribleness is just the dirt on your side of the pane.

Think of it: have you had the experience of going somewhere or touching something, and it "just didn't feel right"? It had some kind of messy, funky vibes on it. It can be that way, too, with food.

That's what kosher and *halal* (laws about the procedures for slaughtering animals and preparing food, in Judaism and Islam, repectively) used to be about. The priest would pray and be entranced and get metaphysically sensitive enough to communicate with and daze the animal about to be slaughtered, at least enough to communicate with it and beg pardon, give thanks and bless that animal for giving up its life to keep the peoples' lives going. Otherwise, the spirits of murdered animals would visit their vengeance upon you and yours who killed and ate them.

On the physiological side, an animal being slaughtered becomes afraid. Fear automatically pumps adrenaline and other chemicals into the animal's muscles. When you eat the meat of a frightened animal, that stuff goes into you, too. There's more: an animal dies because the blood isn't flowing any more to wash away the toxins and poisons the scared cells are creating; each cell chokes on its own cellular waste and suffocates from no oxygen. All the toxins stagnate around those dead cells, and that makes for dirty meat, which makes bad fuel for your body.

A planned diet is also a matter of self-control, of personal strength. That's one reason that yogis abstain from meat, from sex, from movement: control. You can't go on any metaphysical bon voyage if your stomach is telling you to get up and fix it a ha(r)mburger. It's why shamans starve and self-deprive. So, the discipline of vegetarianism has aided me in my growth as a drummer. It has given me a clarity of perception (as I describe in the poem "Sensitive") and commitment that has seen me through to where we are now.

Within four years of seriously starting to drum I felt the need to implement such discipline in my life. I read Dick Gregory and Alvinia Fulton's *Cookin' with Mother Nature;* I prowled through the stacks of D.C.'s YES! bookstore, I listened to the teachings of the Nation of Islam and the Seventh-day Adventists (Adventists lived next door to me in D.C.); I irritated my parents by giving up pork. Then, past irritation, the last day of my junior year of high school was my last day of eating animal flesh.

I read *Back to Eden* by Jethro Kloss, Adelle Davis's *Let's Eat Right to Keep Fit,* and the great, now out-of-print book by Greg Brodsky, *From Eden to Aquarius,* which has chapters on diet, fasting, hydrotherapy, martial arts, yoga, and other aspects of spirituality. Using these and other books I experimented with diets, brewed herb teas for ailments, and, by corollary, became a better cook.

Away from home, I was lucky. I ate the vegetarian meals offered at Oberlin College. I studied biology and physiology to learn the "how" and "why" of the body, and applied that to drumming, too. Upon arrival in New York I sought out like minds, kindred spirits. The path was, for me, no meat, music; open up your soul. I just wish I could see myself then with today's eyes, to perceive what it was that I said that elicited the same response from people, over and over again: "You've got to go check out International." I got a phone number and found out where a drum class was being held. Within two weeks of arrival in New York, I had hooked up with the people I would be working with for the next five years. Everyone was right. The International Afrikan-American Ballet was what I was looking for: hard, authentic training, with a spiritual bent.

My apprenticeship with International went something like this: for my first two years in New York City I went out to Queens every Tuesday night, playing conga, *songba, sekere,* bells, djembe, sticks, and *kutiro* for Olukose's class at the New Horizons Cultural Center in St. Albans. John Blandford was the first dance teacher, a job eventually taken over by other members of the company.

It was tough. From those classes I learned to boost and maintain my energy at the right level, and began to see how the music and the dancing were in symbiosis.

I'd been there about a year when the company instituted a training program for new recruits. I began attending International's rehearsals on Monday, Wednesday, and Thursday nights at the Uhuru Sasa Shule/ Sumner Avenue Armory in Brooklyn as a dancer. A Saturday morning workshop for male dancers and then an afternoon workshop for female dancers were established. I had a tight schedule: aside from attending rehearsals three days a week, I played for Olukose's Tuesday night class, danced and played in the men's dance workshop on Saturday morning for two or three hours, then played for the women's workshop in the afternoon for about the same length of time. At the same time I was working to get a B.F.A. in TV production from New York University. And eventually I did performances. My "premiere" with the company was at the first DanceAfrica program at the Brooklyln Academy of Music in 1978.

Along with this physical stuff I was also working on my diet. When I met my future wife, Vanessa, I was eating peanut butter, honey, and bee-pollen sandwiches. Falafel. And greens. Pretty strong stuff.

I continued my work with herbs. From my rooming-house hovel on Halsey Street I would carry five-pound honey jars full of alfalfa-comfrey-mint tea to IAAB rehearsals and to shows. The alfalfa was to strengthen the nervous system, the comfrey to heal any strain, and the mint to keep us cool, receptive, and harmonious.

I worked steadily with International from 1977 to 1982. Then the devolution of the company, the changing politics of the day, and my own growth demanded I rethink my direction. I committed to the Ausar Auset Society.

"A pan-African religious organization," Ausar Auset was one of the places where my teacher John Blandford suggested I go study. "Brother Ra is deep," John told us, his fledglings, as we sat around after workshop, packed up our clothes, or waited for the bus. "And he gives you the hookups."

What did that mean? Hookups? After a couple of months I sought this place out, the free classes in Harlem given by Brother Ra. My impressions of those early days are a blur to me now; I heard things in Friday night lectures that I always knew but never had articulated. I learned how to separate a Power's manifestation from its cultural baggage. I learned what "Aum" can do. And, as John promised, I did learn the hookups.

I have been a student of history, and of people, all my life. What I found at Ausar-Auset was a framework, a cosmology within which to fit the experiences of my life and the phenomenal world. The teachings of the Ancient Wisdom were what were offered, in a holistic system that encompassed what clothes you wear, what food you eat, what dreams you have, and how you think and act.

We studied the teachings of the Ancients: of the Ayurvedic (pre-Aryan) inhabitants of the Indian subcontinent, of the Khamitians (ancient Egyptians), of the Chaldeans (black inhabitants of the Levant and Mesopotamia), and of the Taoists of ancient China, whose deified ancestors are known as the Dark Ones, too. We alchemized all this study

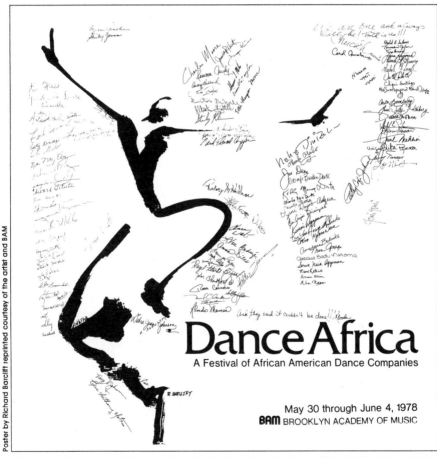

Poster by Richard Barcliff reprinted courtesy of the artist and BAM

Dance Africa
A Festival of African American Dance Companies

May 30 through June 4, 1978
BAM BROOKLYN ACADEMY OF MUSIC

My first performance with International, at the Brooklyn Academy of Music's first DanceAfrica Festival, was an initiation. In the wings, two minutes before we went out on stage, they changed the choreography!

with contemporary African spiritual practices. Delve and you will find these teachings are pieces of one fantastic spiritual system of reunification with the One. They are all parts of the Old Religion, the Yoking that was the Great Mystery sought and destroyed by the Aryans (the people of Ares, of Mars, the god of war). The system scattered and turned into Bacchanalias, into metaphysical meditations, into occult exalted orders, into "voodoo."

In a holistic view of the system, there is yin and yang, Cobra and Vulture, Ha and Tha—for as above, so below. The Great Mother must have her mate. These are the "hookups" John was talking about. How to see the correspondences among Mercury, Hermes, Elegba, Tehuti, Exu, and Ifa. Or among Venus, Aphrodite, Oshun, the Madonna, Auset, and Kuan-Yin. In classes we learned to utilize those images and the powers they represent; we learned about the meaning of mantras and the need for a clean, healthy vehicle (body), for a diet in harmony with the flow of the seasons. Through this work came divination, cosmology, meditation techniques, and trance. And the cognition to use these insights with drums.

THE COMMON AILMENTS OF DRUMMERS

HANDS

Drummers' hands are going to stay hard. On the way to that condition they blister, crack, bleed, and callus. And if you don't take care of the calluses that form, they will cause you to bleed again, or bruise the bones in your hand. So what do you do?

Don't let your flesh become like the wood of the drums' shell—brittle. It will break. Keep your hands supple. Use a light oil, like sunflower or avocado, on your hands before and after playing. Some folks use coconut, some use palm. That's okay, too.

Don't let your calluses build up too high. Toughness doesn't make you better, only perhaps less supple. Get a pumice stone to keep the calluses low. And don't worry about grinding away, it's only dead skin. You'll grow more.

If your hands crack, use the pumice stone to remove the dead skin from the edges of the crack. The wound must be free enough of hard skin to move with flexibility in order to heal.

If your hands blister, leave the blisters unbroken. The body will reabsorb the fluid. If the blister breaks, however, cut the dead skin away. You can get an infection in that moist environment. Take small scissors—I use the ones in my Swiss army knife—and cut the blister off. Let the exposed skin dry a little, then oil it. Keep it oiled and clean. A keratinized layer of skin will form over it for protection. Work to keep this new skin supple with oil. If you don't, you'll get bleeding cracks. You might want to cover the new skin with an adhesive bandage. Take care of your hands, but don't baby them! You have to get back in there and condition the new skin as it's forming to be able to stand the force you are sending through it when drumming.

If calluses get too thick, corns will form. This is dangerous! Corns grow inward and can put pressure on bone or nerve. Should you see a hard, circular area forming in a callus, work hard to get it out. Soak it and pumice it. Expunge it. Otherwise, one day you will be playing and all the force of your stroke will be transfered through that corn into your hand, to the bone. The pain can make you cry.

ARMS

Arms usually become strained after a long or intense session. Get a friend to rub them. Stroke muscles toward the heart for relief. You want to help the body's systems get rid of the toxin buildup that causes you the pain. Of course, for certain nerve and energy work you sometimes massage *away* from the heart. For exactly what *you* need, see a health practitioner. To build upper-body strength, try doing various types of push-ups. Do them with hands under the shoulders, in the center of the chest, with index fingers and thumbs forming a diamond, and with hands and fingers spread wide. Rotate the wrists before and afterward. These different push-ups will build up different sets of muscles you can use for drumming. Push-ups also stretch your chest and upper body, which get tight after playing a little too hard.

BACK

If your back hurts, you've probably been sitting or standing the wrong way. Or perhaps you've been carrying your drum on one shoulder only. You have got to switch sides periodically when you carry that drum, no matter how awkward you feel at first. Otherwise you'll wind up looking like Quasimodo. Remember, no matter what you're doing, the best posture is the most relaxed posture. Reread the Principle on posture on page 36.

BLOOD IN URINE

It's a frightening experience, when after a session you find yourself passing something that looks like grape juice. Some people have told me that it was blood that passed into the system from the beating their hands got. Others have told me it's because of strain on the kidneys or capillaries in the bladder breaking, which bleed into the urine from squeezing the stomach muscles. To date, I do not know what causes it. I have observed that it does follow straining while playing. I know that it definitely happens to djembe players a lot, and sometimes to congeros. But it doesn't have to happen.

The Retreat had already been a good one: a week in the woods communing with Ausar Auset Society members from all over the country. The first couple of days, old friends sat in cabins or the cafeteria, worked side by side, talking up old times. New friends took soft walks through oaks and sycamores to the lake. Children squealed from cabin to cabin. It was a temporary village, city dwellers trying to fill themselves with Earth and close-knit village spirit. Ancestral, mercurial, and venusian invocations (down by the sweet water!) had been successful. But this, tonight, was to be the culmination. It was to be a ritual in the woods, on former planta-tion grounds—a nighttime fireside full-moon invocation of the hot and dry martial force: Mars, Ares, Ogun, Heru Khuti. A new signa-ture rhythm had recently been passed to us from an ancestor, and now, at night, before the fire, was the time to work it out.

Women and men circled the blaze of logs stacked five feet high. Purple and red tie-dye in a herringbone pattern clung to sweaty chests. Chanting Brothers and Sisters reached into baskets full of martial herbs: onions, garlic, peppers. Biting down, they closed their eyes, visualizing the immaturity that must be purged, imbibing spirits, catching Spirit. Spirit flew. Machetes carved the sky, the earth. Fireworks exploded, shocking people inside and outside the circle from complacency into trance and involvement. Those with heavy debts did penance, praying and crying as heat from the fifteen-foot flames baked their moistened faces.

Weaving in and out of all this, dodging sparks and knives and swinging limbs, were one other drummer and I, performing the duty of focusing and binding all the insights and visions of these two hundred people, gathered to turn the flail upon themselves and come clean.

The fire threw stark light and dark. Shadows and people danced. Standing near the blaze, I basked in the heat, then felt sudden cold as Ogun stepped between the fire and me. Rearing back, fat cigar in one hand and broad blade in the other, he points to me, wide-eyed, and then to the drum. I catch my drummate's eye and we lean into it, giving the Spirit and the horse something to really dance to, to shake his head and to laugh at, in a furnacelike way.

We worked the drums that night, spinning to shoot rhythm to those in deep trance, laying back while the deity worked or spoke, but all the while playing, playing, playing. My red-and-white shirt was ripped from my body and draped around my neck. Sparks flew as blades hacked low-burning wood. The sky above the pine forest darkened, then paled. Smoke hung low. More and more participants formed a silent ring about the flames and coals. Voices—some in tongues—spoke low as the fire died down, dawn came closer, and dew took the PING! from the sound of my drum. It was a dynamite ritual.

Exhilarated, steamy with perspiration and rough with soot, I picked my way through the lightening woods to my cabin and the bathroom, expecting to find spalled fingertips and see black tempera flushing through my urethra. After playing Heru Khuti all night at such intensity, what else could one expect? I was wrong; somehow, Spirit had preserved me. My hands, though warm and a little swollen, had no real pain, and there was no blood, from anywhere. It was my experiential version of walking on coals, lying on a bed of nails, or whatever priests do to prove that when in trance there can be no damage. It was deep. I said an extra prayer that night.

If blood in your water does happen to you, don't panic. Just take extra water to flush your system, get some extra vitamin C to quicken healing, and reflect on where your energy was sitting when you were playing that time. Were you tense—the bane of good music and good health? Were you squeezing your abdomen as you played? Sometimes that's good—it gives you extra energy. But if you are continually squeezing, nothing good can come of it. If you were standing, were you bent over? If seated, did you pick up the drum with your legs, or some such? It may take repeated observation to pinpoint the circumstances. Be patient. The watching is also a balm.

PAIN

I have found a great remedy for the pain of bruises and overtaxing of muscles: arnica. The flowers of the plant *Arnica montana* make an excellent medicine for sprains and bruises. I recommend the homeopathic preparation of arnica available in health-food stores and natural pharmacies. Taken orally just after playing, dancing, or other strenuous activity, and then periodically afterwards, an arnica remedy speeds up the healing process so much that it seems nearly to prevent the sprain or bruise from hurting at all. When arnica is taken along with the tissue salt, mag phos, there is even less chance of discomfort.

Arnica also comes in external form, as a liniment. Just rub it on, and it really helps. Not by false heat that expands capillaries—like some over-the-counter ointments—but by actual stimulation of the body's natural healing mechanisms.

PREVENTIVE MEDICINE

HERBS

As I described earlier, I have found that alfalfa, comfrey, and mint in combination work wonders for the overextended musician or dancer. A comfrey infusion can be used as a soothing bath, and the wet leaves can be applied to sore muscles to relieve them.

Of course, when you get deeper into the spiritual aspects of drumming, there are certain energies you will need to imbue yourself with as you do your work. Your progress on this spiritual path can be aided by the use of herbs and their extracts, and with food; the approach works on the same principles as aroma and color therapy. You should speak to someone with experience in dealing with the natural Forces before applying any herbs, scents, oils, or colors. (You'll find a more extended treatment of these concepts under "Deity" in the glossary at the end of this book. The books of Ra Un Nefer Amen listed in the Bibliography are an excellent source of information about these principles.) A discussion of herbs is a good place to raise this tricky question: why do so many drummers smoke? Just the people who need all their wind cut it with tobacco. Well, tobacco is an herb that stimulates one's solar energy—it's associated with the hot and dry solar/melanin force known in Yoruba as Shango and as Heru in the Khamitian pantheon. He is Appllo, Hercules, the Hero, the Heir. He is the drummer's friend; the Man's

Man, who works and plays and fights and loves and rules with vigor. Tobacco stimulates this in a person, so perhaps that is why. But just as milk should be taken as a food, not a beverage, so should tobacco (and alcohol) be used as a medicine, not as a candy or a drug.

BREATHING

Shango/Heru also corresponds to male sexual energy—you know, the Stallion. (That energy is exalted and symbolized in the traditional West African drummer's pants—known as *sokoto, kutiba,* or *daba.* In the U.S. they are worn by two popular Heru men: M. C. Hammer and Bobby Brown.) Here is a breathing exercise that may help you to capture the solar force. Get in the Horse Stance: feet parallel and shoulder-width apart, back straight, and knees bent—ideally with the thighs as close to parallel to the floor as possible. Think how you would be if you were riding a horse.

Reach out in front of you. With arms outstretched, palms down, take a deep breath. I mean a *deep* breath, filling your belly with energy. Breathe to push out your belly below your navel. Then slowly exhale. Repeat.

Then, as you slowly inhale, ball your fists and turn your hands upright, and pull your arms in as if you were pulling back on the reins of a wild mustang. Pull back until the sides of your fists are against your hipbones and your elbows are straight back. And don't raise up out of that Horse Stance squat.

Now breathe out on the count of four, three, two, one; then in, two, three, four. Doing this exercise strengthens your body and imprints in your brain how you should be, posture-wise, when playing. If any of you are martial artists, you'll recognize the principles and practices I discuss. Dancing, fighting, teaching—it's all a practicum on the control and directing of energy.

EXERCISE

If you can't sit up straight, or stand up holding your instrument, what energy will you have to pass on to someone else? Folks must hold their own. Moving your body is one way to get there.

The sports I would most recommend for drummers are swimming and horseback riding. Swimming builds up muscles throughout your body, and it makes the body supple, fluid, and kinetically aware. In the water you know where you are, where your parts are, and how they interact with the medium that surrounds you. Refer again to the poem "Sensitive." The rhythm of strokes, water, and breath envelops your soul. Swimming, with your lungs pushing against the heaviness of water, strengthens your wind.

Riding aids drumming because it demands the focus of your will—into the horse and *with* that of the horse. It teaches you to rule, to be a master in cooperation. You must be strong enough to have your wishes felt and acknowledged, but not brutal to the animal, which will balk. The same lesson carries into cooperation with other people, who will work with you when they can feel what you want, when your drumming

Photo by Marilyn Nance

Baba Ishangi—drummer, dancer, elder—participating in the First Annual Community Baptism for the Afrikan Family. Riis Beach, New York, 1986.

takes them to the place they want to go; but don't push too hard. You may get thrown.

Horses are symbols of solar power, the energy most associated with drummers. It's a force that, when riding, you can feel.

No matter how you do it, exercise will help your drumming. Baba Ishangi, as part of his student drummers' regimen, had the men and women do laps around the studio carrying their drums over their heads, jumping over obstacles and around chairs and such. The Japanese drum ensemble KODO reportedly requires that its apprentices rise every morning at five o'clock to run more than six miles. One of KODO's pieces demanded that "the three players drum in a half-sitting-up position"—that is, the Horse Stance. On the group's last U.S. tour, its members literally ran cross-country, jogging ahead of their truck from coast to coast.

In traditional Africa and the Diaspora, the lives people lived kept them in shape. They rose with the sun, fetched water, walked miles to their fields, worked hard, walked back home, then strapped on the drum and played and danced all night—sometimes for days and nights on end. If you're one of those people who wheeze and "Jeez!" about an hour-long dance class running over, you better eat some bee pollen and work as a furniture mover. Or go out and bike. Put your drum on your chest and do some sit-ups. Put it on your head and do some deep knee bends. To pull down Power you have to have it within, at your command.

Yes! Women play hand drums!! Unfettered by Judeo/Christian/Islamic influence, these young women of southern Africa can strap 'em on, no problem. Notice their relaxed hand technique, and their stance—carrying the weight of the drums in their hips. Compare this to the djembe stance on page 38.

FIVE

Women and Traditional Drumming

Traditional drumming calls out the Sun and the Moon in whoever is doing it. To perform and to persevere in strength and
assurance is to exhibit the qualities of the Sun, the Shango/
Hero/Horus/Heru/Hercules. To endure through time and develop the
internal power to play, to be receptive enough to feel the Spirit's call
and directions about what and how to play to reflect what is going on
within you and what is happening before you is to draw upon the Moon
aspect, the Yemoja/Mother/Mary/Queen/Auset/Isis. In the United
States, unfortunately, the cultural norm is that men ignore their lunar
aspect, and women who act from their solar aspect are considered to be
stepping out of their role. But in fact, whoever is playing music—anyone
who is working for Truth—must have both.

The Western, Judeo/Christian/Islamic tradition, in general, suppresses
females as musicians, save their playing of a few select instruments:
flute, keyboards, and some of the strings. Brass and percussion have
been off-limits to women. Islam, as usually practiced, also downplays
the role of women in music. As that religion spread east into Asia and
south into Africa so did its attendant culture, one that demanded women
stay in their designated place, in the background.

Grateful Dead drummer Mickey Hart, in his book *Drumming at the
Edge of Magic,* speaks of the "African-looking drums" that disappeared

from ancient Egypt's sphere of influence—the Levant and the Mediterranean basin—and from the Celtic lands of the Iberian and Anatolian peninsulas along with worship of the Goddess, as Indo-European culture (shamanism) made inroads. (For a good example of the changes in women's roles that the penetration of the Judeo/Christian/Islamic ethic brought about, read Marion Zimmer Bradley's *The Mists of Avalon*, the story of King Arthur's big sister, Morgan Le Fey.) Hart also notes that just about half of the Old Religion worshipers whom he found depicted with drums were female. And I've got a book (Carl Engel's *The Music of the Most Ancient Nations, Particularly of the Assyrians, Egyptians, and Hebrews; With Special Reference to Recent Discover-*

Female drummers of Khamit, Old Kingdom, 2500 B.C.E. This depiction shows two types of frame drums and, again, one shaped like the Yoruba gudugudu. There were even bones players.

ies in Western Asia and in Egypt. Whew!) that shows the Sisters jammin' on square-frame drums and a frame drum back in . . . I think it's the New Kingdom of Khamit, about two, three thousand years ago. So women drumming is an old documented tradition.

Despite pressure to change, folks in the hinterlands, off the worn paths of acculturation, have somewhat maintained their traditional values. In Saharan Africa, Berber women sit and play the skinned-calabash drum, as do the Peulhs of Senegambia. Still, over here, the idea of women treading in the territory of drumming is frightening to some men. They were taught that men, and only men, were to be drummers. Men play, women dance: simple. Why? I have found no reason why a woman should not do percussion. I do have a word of caution, though. Let's move on.

When you work your muscles, you are burning fuel; your body heats up. To play a drum also takes heat, body heat. Heat that transmutes to movement and then to sound from your instrument made of vegetable and animal matter. The nature of this implement that you're stroking to song so close to your body makes specific demands of you.

What *is* a drum made of? What is it that you are energizing into vibration, into song? Pieces of tree, parts of animal. The manipulation of wood or skin is different from the manipulation of air, reeds, strings, or gut. It commands more of you; it works your whole body. It is about contact: skin is a body's first line of defense, and wood is any tree's skeleton. The invocation of their powers is different from that of pushing air through your lips, or across a dampened reed, or stroking internal organs (gut) with a filimental appendage (hair). Mongo Santamaria said it all when he stated there's something special about that "skin on skin": raw contact. Pulling that fundamental power up and down takes heat.

That fundamental heat is engendered in your lower *tan-t'ien*, down in your pelvic girdle, below and behind your navel, deep inside. From there it goes where you tell it—or where it wants, if you don't control it as it comes up. This is *kundalini,* the twin snakes of the caduceus, Haiti's famous "snake dance," *yanvalou.* Though the Western convention is to fear this energy that is the basis for creativity and sexuality (what did St. Patrick do?), everyone has it. One of life's main lessons is how to work with it for your own and the common good, too. The snake leaves its lair when you drum. It makes you hot inside. It can glide, or it can strike.

A man's gonads are outside his body; they hang there to escape the heat, to be at the optimum temperature to produce more sperm.That is why it is detrimental to a man's health to wear tight clothes and bikini underwear. If the testicles aren't two degrees cooler than the body, sick or weak sperm is made. And the best of a person's nutrients go toward making the next generation—to sperm production in a man and to the growing fetus in a woman. If one doesn't expel the nutrients they are reabsorbed; that's part of the strength derived from temporary celibacy.

A woman's gonads are inside her, kept safe (she holds all the eggs she will ever have—the one's she's born with—in there) and relatively cool. Too much heat in the body, be it from sports overdone, bad eating, bad nerves, or wrong drumming, can fry your eggs. Any questions?

This is not, repeat, *not* to say that women should not play drums. What I do recommend is that women take precautions to safeguard that which cannot be replaced: your generations. How was this done traditionally?

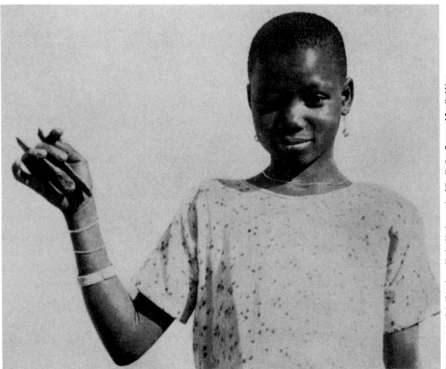

Drums aren't the only percussion: a girl showing her marupa, *or bones.*

Photograph by P.A. Kirby from Musical Instruments of the Native Races of South Africa

Illustration by Oswald Simmonds, Jr., from a photograph by Michel Huet In *The Dance, Art and Ritual of Africa*

Peulh women in Niger play drums for court music.

Over the years I've been collecting every image I can find of traditional drumming by women. In most cases the drum has been in a support of some kind, has had legs of its own, was held to the side, or was held in the lap of the woman. Those who did have drums tied on were young—teenagers—with drums slung around their hips. What can we surmise? You could say it was because the photographers in all the books I've seen were more interested in male drummers, or the society didn't let the camera operator see the female drummers, or it was the wrong time of the year for that. You could say it was a culture's taboos on a woman sitting with her knees apart. Perhaps. But my drumming experience says something else. What is the physiology of it?

A lot of pressure is built up from holding a drum with your legs. Your inner thighs are tense and so is your belly, generating heat. It's stressful. A congero will sometimes pick up the drum with the legs, holding it away from the floor to expand the drum's sound and the stroke's power. As I describe in the chapter "Health and the Drummer," you can drum and find blood in your urine as a result of playing and straining. There is pressure, strong pressure, happening inside. If one isn't careful, male or female, you'll strain yourself. The potential pressure on female organs has to be considered. Think about it.

Sisters, this is just something to consider before you decide which kind of drum to play. If a particular orchestra calls you, investigate all the parts, and remember the kind of shape you have to be in to evoke the energy that drum was designed to carry. Me, I'll only play lead if I have to. If you want to go for it, try to get a stand for your axe. Playing it between your legs would not then strain your belly in the same way. Perhaps slinging it on by a strap around your hips, like a baby on the side, would suit a woman's anatomy. Look at the South African women in the photo on page 96—the way they are standing supports the drum with minimum physical strain. Their legs are wide enough that the drum is free, its weight supported by the pelvis, the center of gravity for women.

Playing drums strapped around the shoulders is a system designed for upper-body-strength men. I'm not saying it can't be done, I'm thinking physics and ease. And (most) men don't have large and/or sensitive breasts to get in the way of the drum straps. Of course, all these considerations are determined by the kind of drum you're talking about and by the kind of body you've got. Often men let a big gut get in the way of playing and the clean flow of energy.

Photo by Hakim Mutluk

Women of the National Dance Company of Senegal change tradition: playing the sabarr *drums in performance.*

In Swaziland women play their version of the berimbau, or diddley bow: the umakweyana.

Musicians: put the common world's exposure to conga and djembe drums aside; there are many other instruments out there that aren't so hard on your body. There are stick drums, like the *kete* of Ashanti (see photo, page 80)or the *jun-jun* of the Mande speakers. There's the Irish *bodhran*. There are the stick-and-hand *sabarr* drums like those played by the women of the Senegalese National Dance Company, who play, by the way, with the drum slung on the side. There are the two-headed drums of South India *(mridangam* and *pakhawaj)* and the *bata* of Yoruba, both played from the lap. Check them out, but remember the social strictures put on women playing those drums, in their original culture. More possibilities? What about the mbira, the "Middle Eastern" *dumbek/durbaka,* the Brazilian *pandeiro,* the trans-savannah *riti* or *halam,* and *berimbau,* the gospel tambourine, or even the down-home bones?

I am *not* saying, then, that women should not play. I *am* asking that you take the concept of physical and metaphysical "heat" into consideration as you check out the world of percussion. Do your research, listen hard. If you're with the Spirit, what can Man say? Be what you decide.

AFTERWORD

Tuesday night, 6:00-9:00! Drum night! I checked my watch, and it looked like once again Ozzie and I were to be the only ones who showed up to play for Olukose Wiles's drum/dance class this week. Olukose's big brother, Herb—the strong, silent type—who taught karate and ran this New Horizons Community Center in St. Albans, Queens, watched us from the office doorway. The trip to New Horizons was a two-subway and one-bus ride that I took every Tuesday night for more than two years, coming first from midtown, then from Harlem, and then from Bed-Stuy. I had to move around a bit my first two years in New York City.

Venette, a Sister from the Virgin Islands with Oshun in her pocket-book—she attracted men just by walking down the street; she'd be *behind* them and they'd turn around—was teaching the usual after-work crew of shape-uppers and Afro-enthusiasts. After a slow hour of warm-ups, late arrivals, and dance-step break-downs, we picked up the pace a taste. After a couple of traces down the floor the fire kicked in, and the class finally started to get hot. Olukose, playing lead on that heavy, Côte d'Ivoire djembe of his, was struggling, straining to pull Ozzie's and my energy levels up enough to support the dancing before us and the lead parts he was playing.

I know my drumming that night was shaky: starting out intense and on time, it would fall behind the group's energy; then I'd notice, bear down, and push my energy back up. I would hold it up for a while, then down it would slip again. I'd know when that happened, 'cause Olukose would start making faces, and I'd have to push past my burning deltoids and tricep muscles, take a deep breath, get in the horse stance and play, play, play! But it would not sustain. I just couldn't get my energy level consistent enough for even output.

Of course by now the place was steaming, and Venette's sweaty feet were leaving prints on the grimy green-and-white linoleum tile floor. She gives the signal, Olukose plays the break, and we've got a moment to chill before going on to *mandianni/domba* (one of the rhythms in "Songba Solo Medley" on *The Drummer's Path* audiocassette/CD). Dripping sweat, panting, and cursing ourselves for not buying juice on our way in, Ozzie and I huddled close to the master to be shown new accompaniment parts.

The teacher sat quietly astride his drum. He sniffed, coughed, and, with bowed head, slowly shook it from side to side. He coughed again, then looked up at us, and rumbled in his cigarette-riddled voice: "Look, I'm coming here straight from work [he did contracting], and I've got kids, five kids, [here he held up his brown-callused hand, fingers out-stretched: five!] that I've got to support. But I'm here every week, and I've got to do this. I've made a commitment to this stuff, to do it right. That's why I'm telling you all this. You've got to play this part like it's the last time you're ever gonna do it, like this is gonna be your last chance to play."

He paused to clear mucus from his lungs.

"And besides," he chuckled, "you never know."

That was food for thought, all right. But what Olukose was trying to express—in his own macabre way—was a solid truth: if you're working with whatever instrument, work it! Get into it for all you and it are worth. Don't waste your time or your life.

Commit. That's the only way to really know the art, the science. Decide to be the best you can, and pull the will and the energy to play out of your guts and let that one drum part, that one piece of the total musical statement, sink down into your spirit and fill you, shake you, rock you. Let it—make *it* breathe *you.*

With time, I got closer to his ideal. Sometimes, when playing, the feeling of the music would just get me rockin'! And I just couldn't help it, and I'd let loose with some extra *ba-ba-boom-ba-booms* on the *songba* drum I was playing. Olukose would instantly—and I mean instantly—

turn on me and bellow, "Play straight! Play straight!" without missing a beat. His meaning: put no embellishments on the drum part he had shared with me.

Afterward, as we packed up and dried off, he explained to us: "You've got to, like, fall in love with that part, that one part, and play it. I mean *really* play it!" One has to absorb the essence of that one rhythm, itself, before going anywhere else. You have to perceive all the part's hidden intricacies and loveliness before you try to step out on it, out of it, or around it.

Like the man said, you've got to love what you're doing, but not just for you. You can take you home and love you. That's not it. You've got to love what you're doing for the playing, for what you and your ensemble fellows make together, and for what can then be done with the energy that you collectively invoke. This is *powerful* juju, not just "performance."

Photo by Sule Greg Wilson

Babatunde Olatunji, symbol of African drumming in the United States for over thirty years. Orisa Conference, New York City, 1986.

If you follow and implement the above guidelines, you will find yourself much more "inside" the music you work with. That in itself is a great reward. But to walk on this path you must embrace discipline, and many things that used to be "fun" won't be anymore. With a new and deeper sensitivity—or even just an inkling—about how the music could optimally function, "jamming" or just plain "getting down" doesn't satisfy anymore.

Look at babies, perfectly happy to babble and babble and babble the day away, content because they have not learned language, true aural communication. But once they have learned, they never go back to babble. The same holds true for learning the language of the Spirit inside you that comes out through the drum. Once you can really talk, you are ashamed to babble; even despite yourself, you can't go home again. Let me show that truth, with this last story:

It was summer 1980. July. I was back in my hometown, D.C., after five years of living in Ohio and New York City. I was pumped up, used to carrying drums and working out; I was looking for someone to play with. It was a hot—whew!—humid, steamy night, and I was driving my daddy's car down near the Navy Yard, craning my neck looking for an Afro Center that an acquaintance had told me of, a place that held dance classes on Tuesday nights.

I'm driving down a tree-lined, nearly deserted street, and then, faintly, I hear it! They're saying, "Come-here-an'-have-so'-fun! Come-here-an'-have-so'-fun! Come-here-an'-have-so'-fun! Come-here-an'-have-so'-fun!"

Adrenaline burns my spine and twists my belly! Instant excitement! Drums! That's it! I hear drums! I twist the car in toward the curb, check my mirrors, U-turn, park it, bounce out of my seat, and am in the place before the echo of the Dodge's screeching wheels can die out against the nighttime cushion of clapboard wood and living trees.

The storefront was bright, and filled with people. A suave brown Sister with big legs and deep dimples was leading the class of fifteen or so young women and three young men. The drummers, playing a variety of instruments, were on the half-balcony above, looking down and getting down.

I stood in the doorway; the outside air caressing my back became cool and refreshing, in contrast with the steamy atmosphere generated by the drummers and dancers inside the refurbished building. Among them I saw someone I knew: one of my old teachers. It was great to see him again. I was in town, and I had connected. Or had I?

The women were dancing lenjengo, *and I tried—oh, I tried!—to rock with where they were putting it. But, inside, I kept repeating: where's the downbeat? Where's the hesitation? Where's the drumstick's* BURRRR! *on the* kutiriba? *Where's the rock? Where's the* funk?

Not there. These people's placement of the rhythm and the dance and mine were from two different levels. What they were doing was outside my experience. In fact, to my ears, it was wrong.

I stayed where I was, near the door. What could I say or do? These people had no context of exposure in which to fit the other rhythms and the intensity that I had learned to rock to. I couldn't school them, but I wanted to.

To me, it wasn't swinging! It wasn't demanding *I get out there and revel in the oneness of movement and sound and floor and air and music and sound and people and drums and spirits and . . . It just wasn't there.*

What I heard was drumming and singing that was slow, messy, weak . . . American-sounding. Not Gambian. More like a cheap imitation. They were working to be in some other place, without coming from their own. So there was nowhere in the music for me, knowing where Seruba's groove is supposed to be, to step in and "get off" on. There was only a (perhaps someday) opportunity to teach these people in the storefront dance class what I had learned of lengengo *and its "feel," of its arrangement, its language, its steps, its stories, its songs.*

I saw the folks were enjoying it: sweating and smiling and kicking their heels. I remained in the door for a while, respected my elder, saluted the drums, thanked my temporary hosts, and returned to the silent night.

I headed back uptown, with the radio off and the window open. My lessons and my foolishness stood face to face, and I observed. I had tried to use what I had learned, out of context, just to have fun and not feel alone. Instead, I discovered that some things just don't translate. In my late-night Tuesday search for drums I had tried to deny something that deep down inside I had already known was true: my "getting off" days were long ago over. That type of "fun" was done.

Everything exacts its price. Amen.

THE PERCUSSIONIST

Man, did I sure once LOVE improvisation!

Sittin' there with the cats
Groovin it, knowin' just where he's gonna go
with his solo

Catchin' that rhythm in the other man's melody
Puttin' it out there
Just so the Brother can lay in on it and get on down!

Here it comes! . . . the gonnagonnagonnagonnagonnagonna
get-it ON!

And we're in a new riff, and I'm back in the groove:

a-Goong, GOOng, . . . Bop! a-Goong, GOOng, . . . Bop! a-Goong, GOOng,
Bop! a-Goong, GOOng, . . .

Wipin' the sweat in time with the music
and pickin' out somebody in the audience just to
watch THEM groove.

That was some slick shit.

But I knew, deep inside, it was deeper than that.
I knew I was deeper than that.

The Stage is a spell.
A matter of Time.

The movers and the shakers/the World Rhythm makers . . .
Those folks ain't pressed on vinyl.

You'll find them in a basement.
You'll meet them in a park.
At a party or a family reunion.
Or maybe even backstage,
Greeting again, secure and rested,
Folks who used to be
Their students.

Their road
Their Truth
Is not in beating and fronting.

Heading to a ritual. Prince Wiliams Forest Park, Virginia, 1984.

It's in guiding spirits
And divining signs
And spreading the Word
And Living It.
And Playing It
Deep inside.
I found them. Or were they sent to me?

GLOSSARY

Afuche. A commercially produced instrument that approximates the sound of a *sekere.* It consists of a corrugated metal cylinder around which is wrapped metal beads. The *afuche*'s handle is at the base of the cylinder.

Akua. An Akan name, meaning "girl born on Wednesday." "Kweku" is a Wednesday-born boy. There is a different energy on each day of the week and each day is ruled by a different planet. The energy of Wednesday is ruled by Mercury.

Amen. Where is this word for ending our prayers from? "Amen," in the Khamitian (ancient Egyptian) language and pantheon, is the Unknown One, God as the humanly inconceivable, the One Beyond. At the end of our supplications to the Greater Force, therefore, we call upon God as the transcendent.

Amer-African. A person born in the Americas whose cultural focus is on his or her African ancestry. These people are a variety of Africans more than they are a variety of Americans.

As-salaam. A greeting in the Arabic language used by Muslims. Like *shalom,* it means "peace."

Ausar. Commonly, and incorrectly, known by the Greek name Osiris, Ausar is the Khamitian deity of perfect equilibrium, of God manifest in man. His color is white; his scent is frankincense; he eats coconut and cocoa butter. He is associated with rebirth and fertility, and therefore with barley, a staple crop of ancient Khamit. He is the god of the Underworld, and of regeneration. For correspondences, examine the story of Lazarus of the Christian Bible (who also rose from the dead) and Obatala of the Yoruba pantheon. (See photo on page 49).

Bata. An orchestra of three hourglass-shaped drums used in the Lucumi religion of Cuba. Cuban *bata* are played with the drum in the lap, one hand playing each head. In Yorubaland, in Nigeria, the *bata* orchestra may consist of five or seven drums, and one head may be played with a leather strip. Today one may buy commercially produced *bata* and hear the music on popular records. (See photo on page 58.)

Bembe. A Santeria (Afro-Cuban) religious ceremony, which includes drums, dance, and song, where one makes offerings to the "gods," confesses one's sins, and receives counsel from those "possessed" by the Deity.

Berimbau. A one-stringed musical bow with a gourd resonator, the *berimbau* is the signature instrument for the Afro-Brazilian martial art of *capoeira*. It is played with a thin, light stick and is accompanied by a small-woven grass shaker, a *caxixi*, that is held in the same hand as the stick. The *berimbau* player directs the action within the *roda*, or circle. The instrument is derived from the *m'bolubumba* of southern Africa. Usually only one *berimbau* is played for *capoeira*. If there are more, there are three parts: *gunga* (bass); *berimbau de centro* (middle), which maintains the rhythm; and *berimbau viola* (high), which plays the variations. Again, the same three-part African aesthetic is in use. *Berimbaus* are pictured on pages 24 and 115. The *berimbau* is featured in "BaKongo Samba" on *The Drummer's Path* audiocassette/CD.

Bodhran. A traditional Irish/Celtic frame drum resembling a large tambourine. The bodhran is played in a loose-wristed manner with the index finger or a small mallet known as a tipper.

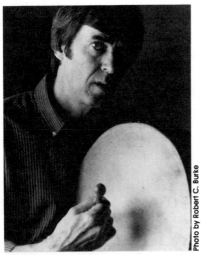

Euro-Americans don't have to look to Africa for drums: the Irish bodhran. Pictured at left is Celtic Thunder's bodhran player, Jesse Winch.

Photo by Sule Greg Wilson

This photograph, taken at the 1990 Batizado (baptism) of new capoeiristas, clearly shows the difference in size and thickness of the three components of the berimbau orchestra. Synod Hall, Cathedral of St. John the Divine, New York City, 1990.

Bolon. A three-stringed harp of the Malinke people. It was known as a war drum because it led soldiers into battle, and its gourd resonator was played as a drum; its strings are plucked, as well.

Brekete. A two-headed, stick-played drum of West Africa. Common to the Dagomba of northern Ghana, this thin-shelled, thin-skinned, snared drum is now played by other peoples of savannah Africa. See page 76 for an illustration of the Brekete drum.

Buba. A flowing overgarment worn by men and women in savannah Africa. (See photo on page 12).

Capoeiristas. Practitioners of the Afro-Brazilian martial art called *capoeira* (pronounced cahp-oh-air-ah). *Capoeira* is a potentially lethal form that includes sweeps, handstands, and moves inspired by animals to down opponents. Effective against slave catchers, *capoeira* was outlawed, so the martial art was made to look like a dance: folks practicing this deadly art appeared to be dancing peacefully to the drums and *berimbau* as the police cruised by.

Chakra. Sanskrit for "wheel." Chakras are energy centers of the body. Each has a specific function in one's spiritual growth and awareness. According to Ra Un Nefer Amen there are fourteen major chakras.

Chant. Chanting, as used in the context of this book, means more than mere song or melody. It means sacred music, songs for the Spirit. Traditional functional music is often "invocation music," whose arrangement of notes activates specific centers of the brain, and whose lyrical poetry invokes images that reinforce and stimulate the altered states of awareness brought about through the melody and the rhythm.

Chi. Also written "ki," this is your life force, your bioenergy.

Clave. (Pronounced CLAH-vay.) From the Spanish *llave,* or "key." The clave is the basic beat, or pattern (played on bell, sticks, or sometimes on drum, body, or hand), around which the rest of the music/rhythm is structured. It is the "key" into the *character* of the music, rhythmically and melodically. It's not just a down beat; if you recognize the clave, you know what that basic "feel" of the music is, no matter how different the drumming or other instrumentation may be. The clave is the music's foundation, its heartbeat. For example, when you hear, "One, two, *cha-cha-cha!* One, two, *cha-cha-cha!*" you know what the dance is, where the "groove" is. It's the same way with the *oom, pah-pah, oom, pah-pah* of a waltz: when you hear the "clave" of the waltz, you know what the songs will be like. You can picture the scene: the swish of full dresses, the bows of the men. The same kinds of associations happen when one hears the "*one!* and . . . three, two, *one!* and . . . three, two, *one!*" of a Lamba from Mali or Guinea. Or the *one,* two . . . one, two, three of rumba guaguanco. You know where it's at; that's the "clave." Clave is also the name of an instrument—two hardwood sticks approximately eight inches long; their sound is sharp.

Conga drum set Counterclockwise from right: tumbao, quinto, and conga.

Conga. The most commonly played hand drum in the United States today. The conga evolved in Cuba from Old World styles of drum, dance, and song, and became popular in the United States with the Afro-Cuban jazz movement of the 1940s.

Coro. The chorus of an Afro-Cuban religious ceremony.

Deity. Deities are not "gods," but rather are a form of recognition of God's multifarious manifestation. For the world to function in harmony, for each thing to have its "place in the sun" and not crash into the next one, there must be order.

Science demonstrates that, in nature, there is a basic septenary (seven-level) system of energy in the world. There are the seven levels of the periodic table of the elements and the twenty-eight-day lunar cycle that breaks down into seven-day weeks. Or maybe you are the seventh son, or you've been lucky enough to be in seventh heaven.

This division functions on many different levels: colors, scents, herbs, minerals, and animal and human temperament. African peoples, and others, have recognized this division of natural forces. Named deity, *orisa*, angel, saint, or bodhisattva, such a force is a personification of a particular level of energy of the world. All phenomena—color and scent, the thought behind a movement, the day of the week, or a chemical element—are in harmony and correspondence with one of these natural forces; they must be, in order to fulfill their role in this world and not get in the way of the rest of Nature.

If you have heard of the seven African powers—*Los Siete Potencias*—seen someone with beads of seven different colors, or studied the old astrology that recognized seven basic planetary influences, you have come across instances of working within the ancient system of order.

Remember, no two things can occupy the same space at the same time; there are natural laws for that. The deities, the forces, are names for those laws. Don't worry if someone else considers this "idol worship" or "voodoo." So, too, were scientists doubted when Western Europe became consciously part of the world community. Some folks recognize that we must work in complement with the world; some don't realize that anything else is conflict. Anything else *is* conflict.

Diaspora. From the Greek term *diaspeirein*—dispersion—"diaspora" means the scattering of a people; in this case, the dispersion of Africans due to the European and Arab business of selling people as chattel, unpaid labor. The African Diaspora includes India and far Asia, the Mediterranean and Western Europe, and the Americas.

Diddley bow. An indigenous U.S. one-stringed instrument.

Djembe. The chalice-shaped drum found among the Mande-speaking peoples of West Africa. The carrying power of the djembe's sound and the high energy it invokes in players and audiences make it an extremely popular hand drum in the United States. (See photo on page 10.)

Photo by Sule Greg Wilson

Ashanti drum ensemble at the 1976 Festival of American Folklife in Washington, D.C. Note the donno on the right.

Some have said that the djembe goes back to the Old Mali empire and has been spread by the trade and empire building of the Mande people. Anthropologist and percussionist Doris Green, inventor of Drumnotation, says that long ago the ensemble was called the *songba* orchestra, after the time- and clave-keeping instrument, rather than djembe, and that the djembe itself was born in the forest regions of Sierra Leone.

Donno.   An hourglass-shaped "talking drum" used by the Ashanti of Ghana and popular among the Dagomba of the northern part of Ghana. Squeezed under the arm to change the drum skin's tension, the frame of the *donno* is relatively lightweight and narrow, which gives it a high-pitched sound.

Dun-dun.   The hourglass-shaped "talking drum" of the Yoruba of Nigeria. Made with thick thongs, which are manipulated by the hand to produce the different tones, the *dun-dun* has a more "rounded" sound than the *donno*.

Gallop.   The common U.S. term for a middle or accompaniment part on hand drums. It sounds just like its name (it's onomatopoeic). To feel the rhythm of the gallop: count one, two, three, four; one, two, three, four; one, two, three, four, and so on. Then say "gallop" instead of "one" and "three." That will give you an idea of the sound.

Geechee. Africans and Afro-Indians living in proximity to the Ogeechee River of Georgia. Geechees have distinctive folkways and dialect and are thought of synonymously with the "low country" people known as Gullah. Gullah "bush dialect" was featured in the film *Glory*, albeit badly. Also see **Gullah.**

Great Darkness. The nothingness that is the potential for all. Think of science—a black hole swallows *everything*, so anything can be found within it. So also with the internal, unknown realm of each person's spirit. The term "subconscious" is an attempt to define part of this.

G.R.H.S. God Rest His Soul; a ritual phrase used when speaking of those who have passed on.

Guaguanco. A rhythm and dance from Cuba. A "country" tradition, this dance takes much of its form from the courtship dance of a rooster and hen. A form of rumba, *guaguanco* is a standard conga rhythm; it is featured on *The Drummer's Path* audiocassette/CD.

Gullah. A shortening of "Angola," Gullah is an Amer-African language spoken in the low country and sea islands of the Carolinas and Georgia. The language and folkways of these people have been the subject of numerous studies, notably Lorenzo Dow Turner's *Africanisms in the Gullah Dialect.* The term can also refer to the people themselves. Also see **Geechee.**

Heru (Horus). A person's solar power, found in the color orange, in citrus fruits, horses, garnet, in the will, and the gonads. Heru the Hero, the Heir, fights tirelessly for what is correct and best for all. He shines as the sun, on everyone. This Khamitian personification corresponds to Shango of the Yorubas. Aspects of him are in the Hercules, Jesus, and Sundiata legends.

Heru Khuti (Greek: Ra-Herakte). Khamitian name for martial, warrior, Shaka Zulu energy: iron and steel, hot peppers, strong drink, fire, muscles, and red eyes. Heru Khuti is "the trailblazer," the force that kills the evils people do. It corresponds to Ogun (Yoruba), Tigare (Akan), or Ares/Mars. We all know what hotheads they are.

Het Heru (Hathor). See Oshun.

Hetep. Khamitian for peace and blessings, or to live in harmony with God/ Nature in all manifestations.

Homeopath. A person who practices homeopathy, using infinitesimal dosages—often little greater than an electromagnetic signature—of remedies that stimulate the body's own natural defenses, resources, and systems to overcome disease. Contemporary Western medicine is mostly allopathic, attacking the disease itself with large enough doses of drugs to "cure" the patient.

Iya. The largest, deepest, lead drum of the *bata* orchestra. The word means "mother." Also see **Bata.**

Juju.   Manipulation of electromagnetic forces via one's will and the use of animal, vegetable, and mineral matter. West African "magic," or "hoodoo." Also see **Wanga.**

Jun-jun.   A large two-headed drum made of wood or, more recently, of oil cans. In the djembe orchestra it is used to accent and call changes and maintains musical integrity. The jun-jun is a contrabass instrument and is featured on "Jun-jun Lamba" on *The Drummer's Path* audiocassette/CD. (See photo on page 10.)

Ka.   The Khamitian name for one's complex of behaviors, one's personality. Corresponding to the ninth sphere of the Kabala's Tree of Life, it is the seat of memory, of learning on the physical plane. See the book *Metu Neter,* by Ra Un Nefer Amen, for an excellent and extensive treatment of this concept.

Kabalistic.   Referring to the Kabala, the ancient Chaldean system of classification of physical and metaphysical phenomena. Note: Kabalistic thought is a product of the Chaldeans, black people. For more information about Kabala and its origins, see the writings of Herotodus, as well as Ra Un Nefer Amen's *Metu Neter* and Ivan Van Sertima's *African Presence in Early Asia.*

Kundalini.   The psychic energy one becomes aware of in "fight-or-flight" situations, *kundalini* is one's most powerful spiritual energy. It manifests as sexual energy and is seen as the paired "snake gods" (Iyawedo and Damballawedo) of Haitian Yanvalou, the twined serpents of the caduceus carried by Mercury, the "fertility python" (Domba) of the Lemba people, and Shango's thunderbolts.

Kundu.   Ki-Kongo for "navel," this word connotes the generative force of the belly, one's root chakra, or *kundalini.*

Kofi.   Akan name for a boy born on Friday. Kwame is a Saturday-born boy. Also see **Akua.**

Kutiro.   An orchestra of three drums played stick-and-hand by the Mandinka people of the Gambia. The *kutiro* orchestra—*kutiraba, kutirindingo,* and *sabaro*—plays for ceremonies and social events.

Lamba.   A Bambara/Manding rhythm (with its accordant songs, dances, clothes, talismans, and so forth; see **Clave,** above) played at rituals of major passages in life—marriage or circumcision, for example.

Lenjengo.   A lively recreational dance performed by the Mandinka of Senegambia. Kutiro drums accompany the dance.

Mandianni.   A Bambara/Manding rhythm (as **Lamba,** above) played at festive occasions.

Manding.   Also known as "Mande," Manding are any of the people related as a cultural group who speak Mande-derived languages. Manding people reside, generally, within Mali, Senegambia, Cote d'Ivoire, Guinea, Burkina

Faso, Sierra Leone, and Liberia. These are the descendants of the founders
and rulers of the Ghana, Mali, and Songhai empires that existed at least as
early as the eighth century and lasted through about the sixteenth century.
One of the major ethnic groups of West Africa, their part in the African
Diaspora, and therefore all American culture, is immense.

Mandinka. A Mande-speaking ethnic group of the Gambia. The Kutiro drum
orchestra is part of their tradition.

Mantra. A primal sound, one of the basic rates of vibration that make up
the physical and metaphysical world.

Mbira. A keyboard instrument found throughout Africa. The mbira *(deze,*
sanza, likembe, kalimba) consists of a soundboard, resonator box or gourd,
and metal or reed keys that are plucked with fingers, thumbs, or both. (See
illustrations on page 122.)

Melanin. A honey-gold pigment that is responsible for the color of one's
hair and skin. A kindred chemical, melatonin, resides in the pineal gland and
is responsible for the absorption of solar energy. The presence of melanin
in the nervous system has been said to aid in intuition and psychic ability.

Photo by Sule Greg Wilson

U.S. style Kutiro *orchestra, developed by Obara Wali Rahman on* sabaro *(lead) drum (center), with*
Olukose Wiles (left) on kutiriba *(bass) and Walter Ince on* kutirinding. *Klitgord Auditorium,*
Brooklyn, New York, 1978.

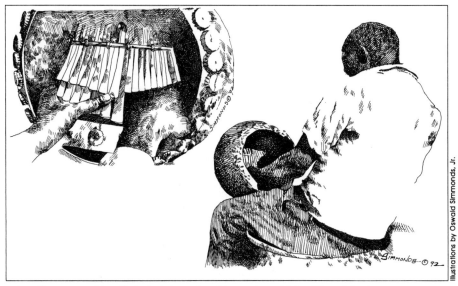

Illustrations by Oswald Simmonds, Jr.

Mbira (deze, sanza, likembe, kalimba), as played in southern Africa. The calabash acts as a resonator, increasing the volume of the instrument.

Meridians.   Channels through which one's *chi,* or life force, flows. The flow of energy through meridians is what is manipulated when one receives acupuncture treatment.

Mridangam.   A two-headed drum of India, more popular in the south (as compared to the tabla *bayan,* more popular in the north).

Mudram.   Sanskrit word denoting a posture or series of postures, a form of dance that instills a specific state of consciousness, trance, or heightened sensitivity.

Nephesh.   A Chaldean term denoting the part of the spirit that animates, that allows one to move. The *nephesh* acts automatically in danger, anger, fear, or habit. It is animal, the part of your spirit trained through repetition and ritual. It's Western correspondent is the astral light.

Nonmelanized.   People with no melanin (white people). Also see **Melanin.**

Obatala.   See **Ausar.**

Ogun.   See **Heru Khuti.**

Orisa.   Derived from *ori,* meaning "head" in the Yoruba language. The *orisa* are the deities, the angels, the gods of the Yoruba. See **Deity.**

Oshun.   Yoruba name for the power of harmony, joy, music, sexiness. She loves gold and orange. In Khamit (ancient Egypt) she is Het-Heru, whom the Greeks called Hathor. In the West she is called Freya, Bridgit, Venus, or

Aphrodite. Her day is Venus-day, Freya-day, Vendredi, Friday. (See photo on page 50.)

Other Side.   The spirit world.

Performance.   Let's break this word down. The prefix "per-" means "through" or "by way of." The second syllable, "form," means "a recognizable structure," a form. So when you "perform," you do something or express something by using a structure, be it movement of body or air molecules or light or other energy. If another person knows the language of symbols you are using, or is intuitive, he or she will recognize the patterns and then think or feel something as a reaction to them. Then there is communication.

Quica.   A friction drum, the "lion's roar." This drum has a stick or string attached to the underside of the drum head. When dampened and stroked, the stick sends the vibrations into the drum head. The drum squeaks, or roars.

Quinto.   The highest-pitched, smallest drum of the conga orchestra. (See illustration on page 116.)

Riney.   A reddish skin and hair tone.

Rumba.   An Afro-Cuban rhythm, a basic form of Afro-Cuban folk dance.

Sabarr.   An orchestra of hand-and-stick drums of the Wolof people of Senegal, consisting of (from lowest to highest) the *goron, lamba, mbalak,* and *sabarr* drums. (See photo on page 103.)

Santeria.   An Afro-Cuban religion in which, over time, the *orisa* of the Yoruba people have been amalgamated, somewhat, with the saints of the Catholic church. Santeria and similar syncretic religions have millions of adherents in the African Diaspora.

Segundo.   The second drum in a conga-drum orchestra.

Sekere.   A Yoruba word, pronounced SHAY-ke-reh. The instrument *sekere* is a calabash gourd surrounded with a net, which has beads strung into it along its entire length. The player manipulates and strikes the gourd, causing the net to move and strike the beads against the sides of the calabash. (See photos on pages 58 and 61 and listen to "Calabash" on *The Drummer's Path* audiocasette/CD.)

Sekher.   Khamitian name for the Power of Time, Cronos. As no two things may exist in the same space in the same time, Sekher/Saturn regulates this. Death creates matter, energy, and space for new life, symbolized in the Yoruba Babaluaye, "god of smallpox," and the Hindu Kali, who wears a necklace of fifty skulls. Time, the great equalizer, is on your side—if you learn to work with it.

Shiko.   Also, and correctly, *Ashiko.* A straight, cone-shaped hand drum, originally from Nigeria, popular in the United States. Chief Bey tells me that *bata* derived from the *ashiko* drum.

Siete Potencias, Los. "The Seven African Powers." Los Potencias are associated with certain herbs, colors, and Catholic saints. They are looked upon as personifications of natural forces that can be brought to bear to better one's life. See *Jambalaya* by Luisah Teish (listed in the Bibliography) for more information.

Songba. The double-headed bass drum of the djembe orchestra. The *songba* is played two-handed: one hand plays the drum head with a stick, the other hand plays a bell, setting up polyrhythms. (See illustration on page 77.)

Tabl. Generic Arabic word for a drum. Compare the Indian "tabla" or European "tabor."

Tama. The hourglass-shaped "talking drum" of the Wolof of Senegal. The *tama* is very small and is played up under the armpit.

Photo by Sule Greg Wilson

Members of the folkloric troupe Les Peulhs du Senegal accompany their vocalist with the tama *pressure drum. New York, 1986.*

Tambora. A two-headed drum that is the heart of Dominican merengue music.

Tan-t'ien. Just as there is a circulatory system for your blood, there is also a circulatory system for your body's energy. These channels of energy, called meridians, are what are manipulated when you undergo acupuncture treatment. *Tan-t'ien* is the Chinese name for the three main energy-processing centers of the human body. Your *tan-t'ien,* or "stoves," transform (or "cook") your energy to subtler forms, higher wavelengths. Your food/chemical and animal/sexual energy (*ching/king*) is transformed into life, or human/moral energy (*chi*), then up into metaphysical spiritual energy (*shen*). Think of ice to water to cloud, or wood to energy and ash. The lower *tan-t'ien,* the Bantu *Kundu,* is your *kundalini* spot.

Trini. A native of Trinidad.

Tua-u. Khamitian word meaning "many thanks."

Tumbao. Also known as *tumba* or *tumbadoro,* the *tumbao* is the bass drum of the conga drum orchestra.

U.S.ans. Citizens of the United States of America. "American" is a generic term that denotes anyone from Alaska to Tierra del Fuego. "U.S.ans" is specific.

Veve. Sacred writing done at Vodun ceremonies. The intricate drawings, usually executed on the ground in cornmeal, are said to be the "gates" to the "gods."

Wanga. Also spelled "ouanga," this is the practice of using physical and psychical forces to influence people and the physical world; it is magic, occult science. The same term is used for a metaphysical power pack, a *mojo,* a hand, a receptacle for occult energy.

Wolof. The dominant ethnic group of the nation of Senegal in West Africa. The Wolof states were among the first to trade with sailing Europeans in the 1400s.

Yantra. A Sanskrit word meaning a design or pattern that invokes a certain state of consciousness, trance, or heightened sensitivity. Like the cornmeal drawn designs of Vodun (see **Veve**).

Yoruba. A traditional nation and an ethnic group within the modern nation of Nigeria, their metaphysical classification system has greatly influenced Diaspora African religions.

Zogginated. When a recipe, orchestra, or relationship has a chance to "set" and all the components have worked their way into optimum harmony.

SELECTED BIBLIOGRAPHY

Books on drumming are few and far between. In a way, that is as it should be, for drumming is an oral and aural experience. Much of what drumming *is* cannot be put on paper. It is the feeling, the invocation, that is the message of the music. You can only get that by encountering the real thing. But having some background may center you as you try to become technically proficient and spiritually receptive enough to get the most you can out of each situation out there in the world. These books can help set you up for that receptivity, if you use what they have to say. Open yourself.

Almeida, Bira. *Capoeira: A Brazilian Art Form. History, Philosophy, and Practice.* Berkeley, CA: North Atlantic Books, 1986. This book by a master practitioner (Almeida's title is Mestre Acordeon) is one of the few sources in English on this dynamic martial art. Through words, photos, and notation Almeida offers history and folklore and demonstrates how vital music is to *capoeira*'s existence. As you read, remember that there is the old tradition (*capoeira angola*) and the crossover style (*capoeira regional*).

Amen, Ra Un Nefer. *Black Woman's, Black Man's Guide to a Spiritual Union.* Bronx, NY: Oracle of Thoth, 1981. This book is the best one I have found for putting traditional African sensibility and cosmology into a daily living context.

_____ . *Health Teachings of the Ageless Wisdom.* Vol. I. *Fundamental Principles.* Bronx, NY: Oracle of Tehuti, 1983. This book documents the necessity of eating, sleeping, fasting, and performing life's functions in harmony with the cycles of the world. It explains the Tetragrammaton, the Four Temperaments, and offers insight on homeopathy. A must.

_____. *Meditation Techniques of the Kabalists, Vedantins, and Taoists.* Bronx, NY: Maat Publishing, 1976. This book "gives you the hookups." It gives what most hatha-yoga classes don't—a "why" for the positions you are doing. It tells you which glands or chakras are being stimulated. It introduces *pranayama* (breathing techniques), the fuel for yoga's effectiveness. It explains the difference between *jnana, karma,* and other yogas. It breaks down Kabala to a practicable system, sans speculations. It explains the Tree of Life. Get it.

_____. *Metu Neter: The Great Oracle of Tehuti and the Egyptian System of Spiritual Cultivation.* Bronx, NY: Khamit Corporation, 1990. This is, honestly, the most complete book on spirituality out there. It breaks down the cosmology referred to in *The Drummer's Path* and offers step-by-step guidance on traveling one's road. It gives excellent background into African spirituality and the use of visualization and the power of breath. A must for anyone seriously interested in Egyptology. *Metu Neter* means "The Word of God" in the Khamitian language.

(The four books by Ra Un Nefer Amen mentioned above can be ordered through Khamit Corporation, P.O. Box 281, Bronx, NY 10462. The Amen books are pretty dense, and the writing style is difficult if you're not familiar with the subject matter. Be sure to read Mbiti, Castaneda, Thompson, and Keyes for an introduction to the concepts explored in detail by Amen.)

Bebey, Francis. *African Music: A People's Art.* New York: Lawrence Hill, 1975. This is one of the few books that gives an authoritative overview of the continent's music cultures. Bebey, a Cameroonian, describes the music and those who make it in the context of their function in society. The material is socioanthropological, yet written in a popular style. As the book's cover states, it is profusely illustrated, with an excellent, if dated, discography. The descriptions of instruments are broken down by type, so if you have a question about something you are playing, or thinking of playing, you can find it. But read the whole book. It will help you understand the "why" of African, and African Diaspora, music.

Berliner, Paul F. *The Soul of Mbira: Music and Traditions of the Shona People of Zimbabwe.* Berkeley, CA: University of California Press, 1978. I wish we could have a book like this for every instrument we were interested in. Berliner investigates and describes the history, spirituality, tradition, technology, and technique of these beautiful voices of god. His book should be read to understand just how deep the learning of an instrument can get. Well-illustrated and -annotated, *The Soul of Mbira* notes recordings that supplement the text. Mbira music is included on the *The Drummer's Path* audiocassette/CD.

Castaneda, Carlos. *The Teachings of Don Juan: A Yaqui Way of Knowledge.*

Berkeley, CA: University of California Press, 1968. This book was the introduction to the ways of the shaman for many, many people. Folks interested in the ways of Spirit, or people with Indian blood, should read this book. Some say it is a hoax. But some of the stuff Castaneda speaks of works; at least for me. Hetep.

Chia, Mantak, with Michael Winn. *Taoist Secrets of Love: Cultivating Male Sexual Energy.* New York: Aurora Press, 1984; Chia, Mantak, and Maneewan Chia. *Healing Love Through the Tao: Cultivating Female Sexual Energy.* Huntington, NY: Healing Tao Books, 1986. Drumming is about generating energy. The body is the generator, the sex glands the nuclear pile. These books will help you learn to use it.

Courlander, Harold. *A Treasury of Afro-American Folklore: The Oral Literature, Traditions, Recollections, Legends, Tales, Songs, Religious Beliefs, Customs, Sayings, and Humor of Peoples of African Descent in the Americas.* New York: Crown Publishers, 1976. This companion to Courlander's *A Treasury of African Folklore* is as chock-full as the subtitle makes it sound. It also has photos of drums and drummers, and it compares the African and the Diaspora versions of stories and folkways. A good sourcebook.

Diallo, Yaya and Mitchell Hall. *The Healing Drum: African Wisdom Teachings.* Rochester, VT: Destiny Books, 1989. When I read this book I was shocked. So many of the things that happened to Mr. Diallo in his village in Mali were lessons I experienced over here in the States and in Africa. The book and its accompanying tape give a glimpse of the traditional world, a world that is shrinking every day, yet will live and expand if we live by its tenets: harmony and sympathy, wherever and whoever we are.

Emery, Lynne Fauley. *Black Dance in the United States from 1619 to Today.* Rev. ed. Princeton, NJ: Princeton Book Company, 1988. You may say you're interested in *drumming,* not dance. Well, *Black Dance* tells the story of the development of African culture in the United States and the Caribbean, through that one topic—and if you want to play music, you should know how the music was used, and what for, neh?

Epstein, Dena J. *Sinful Tunes and Spirituals: Black Folk Music to the Civil War.* Urbana, IL: University of Illinois Press, 1977. This book is full of surprises, such as a photo from the British Museum of an Akan drum collected in Virginia in the eighteenth century. This is the same story as Emery's *Black Dance,* but from a complementary slant. A person needs to be respectful and know all they can about the folks who died on the soil where they live.

Hart, Mickey, with Jay Stevens. *Drumming at the Edge of Magic: A Journey into the Spirit of Percussion.* San Francisco: Harper, 1990. Hart's book offers the Western insight into the world of percussion. It details science's approach to cultures with a drumming tradition and describes Hart's lifelong romance with rhythm. It shares ways of learning the drum from different parts of the world. Nevertheless, I do take issue with the discussion at the end of the book, where Hart Eurocentrically ascribes to Western culture (his heritage) both the Mother Goddess/Spirit Possession/drumming tradition *and* the shamanistic tradition that tried to destroy it.

· Hayden, G. and D. Marks, eds. *Repercussions: A Celebration of African-American Music.* London: Century Publishing, 1985. For those who missed the series "Repercussions" on PBS, get this book. *Repercussions* bounces back and forth across the Atlantic, from Gambia to Georgia, from the Caribbean to modern Highlife, giving you a survey of the commonality of African music.

Holloway, Joseph E., ed. *Africanisms in American Culture.* Bloomington, IN: Indiana University Press, 1990. This book was fun, giving me documentation for things I had felt intuitively long before. "If traditional African religion celebrates and affirms human life, with God as the apex of being and humankind as the center or pivotal point, it could also function thusly for Gullah slaves in the New World." Thank you. Of course the book talks of Africanisms in New World music and of the Kongo influence in American culture. But the real eye- and ear-opener is the essay "The African Heritage of White America," by John Edward Philips. Much more than Elvis, I'm telling you.

Howard, Joseph H. *Drums in the Americas.* New York: Oak Publications, 1967. This is the drum information bible. It tells you about Amerindian, European, African, Asian, and American "mulatto" drums and percussion instruments. It tells you the names of drum orchestras and when and where they played. And it even has photographs of the drums and the sticks to play them with. It's a hardback platinum mine.

Huet, Michel. *Les Hommes de la Danse.* Lausanne, Switzerland: La Guilde du Livre, 1954. This is a picture book. If anyone has seen *The Dance, Art, and Ritual of Africa* by the same author, you will have an idea of this one. *Les Hommes de la Danse* gives you a whole photo essay of a ceremony, instead of just one or two images as the other book does. The photographs are also in black-and-white, so the content is easier to study.

Jahn, Jahnheinz. *Muntu: An Outline of the New African Culture.* New York: Grove Press, 1961. This book is a standard college text, and though it may be old, it is an excellent introduction to the African cosmological framework. When I first read it, I went crazy on the first sentence: "Africa is entering world history." But I persevered and learned a lot.

Keyes, Ken, Jr. *Handbook to Higher Consciousness.* Fifth ed. Marina del Rey, CA: Living Love Center, 1975. This book offers exercises and philosophy that can start one on a spiritual path, no strings attached.

Lucas, J. Olumide. *The Religion of the Yoruba: Being an Account of the Religions, Beliefs, and Practices of the Yoruba Peoples of Southern Nigeria, Especially in Relation to the Religion of Ancient Egypt.* Lagos, Nigeria: C.M.S. Bookshop, 1948. This book is nearly impossible to find, but, as the title says, it helps to put the ancient world and the modern one, its heir, into perspective.

Mason, Bernard Sterling. *How to Make Drums, Tomtoms and Rattles: Primitive Percussion Instruments for Modern Use.* New York: Dover Publications, 1974. An excellent book on the folklore and manufacture of Native American drums and percussion instruments, originally published in 1938. The language is dated, but the information can't be beat.

Mbiti, John S. *African Religions and Philosophy.* Garden City, NY: Anchor Books, 1970. If you want to know what drums call down, you must understand, intellectually, the hierarchy of the Spirit. Mbiti offers a beautiful survey work of this topic. This is a standard college text.

Nketia, J. H. Kwabena. *Our Drums and Drummers.* Accra, Ghana: Ghana Publishing House, 1968. This book is a wonderful introduction to the percussion orchestras of a single nation, Ghana. Dr. Nketia, a respected African author, shows the styles and instruments of the different ethnic groups of his nation, a reality rarely understood by those across the waters. The book also is very well illustrated with photographs.

Stearns, Marshall Winslow, and Jean Stearns. *Jazz Dance: The Story of American Vernacular Dance.* New York: Macmillan, 1968. The Stearns' book, described on the cover as "a history of dancing to jazz, from its African origins to the present," is *the* book on U.S. African-American dance. To honor the drumming tradition of the United States, you must know what it was that forced and shaped its development: U.S. African dance. John Bubbles was credited with inventing be-bop, because of where he was coming from with his dancing. What made Bojangles special? What was the era that the death of Sammy Davis, Jr., was the end of? Read this book.

Stoller, Paul, and Cheryl Olkes. *In Sorcery's Shadow: A Memoir of Apprenticeship Among the Songhay of Niger.* Chicago: University of Chicago Press, 1987. This book is the Songhay counterpart to Castaneda's *Teachings of Don Juan.* It lets you feel what it is like to enter a Spiritual World, where everyone around you is hooked into the cosmos, consciously, and knows ways to work it.

Stuckey, Sterling. *Slave Culture: Nationalist Theory and the Foundations of Black America.* New York: Oxford University Press, 1987. This book breaks U.S. African history into categories determined by the real movers and shakers of U.S. African culture, folks like David Walker, Henry Highland Garnet, and Paul Robeson. *Slave Culture* honors those who maintained their African traditions despite the penalties. It offers proof that Africans never gave up their African selves, even if the form had to change. And it talks about drums.

Teish, Luisah. *Jambalaya: The Natural Woman's Book of Personal Charms and Practical Rituals.* San Francisco: Harper 1985. The book gives you rituals, stories, charts, and tables; it gives you cosmology. You know, the hookups. It's a good book to read to start getting closer to the power we and those around us have. It complements Amen's books. And it is reminscent of *The Drummer's Path* in its use of illustrative anecdotes.

. Thompson, Robert Farris. *African Art in Motion: Icon and Act.* Los Angeles: University of California Press, 1979. This book is vital to anyone who wants to understand African aesthetics. In their own words, natives of particular cultures describe the meanings in their art. Why does a king wear gold? What is the symbology of red? When a sculpture depicts a bent knee, what is it saying? How do you tell the rank of one saluting the drums? If you ever wondered what you were looking at in a museum, beyond what the label tells, read this book, which was published in conjunction with the Frederick S. Wright Art Gallery and the National Gallery of Art.

. _____. *Flash of the Spirit: African and Afro-American Art and Philosophy.* New York: Random House, 1983. This collection of essays informs in depth. Where did the words "jazz" and "funky" come from? Why do U.S. African graves have bottles and shells on them? What are the connections between the ancient Dahomey kingdom and modern Haiti? What are the correspondences between Yoruba, Fon, and Haitian names of deities, and how did Europeans miss the point in their ethnographic studies? What is *ashe*? Do musicians invoke this, and who controls it? Why are snakes carved on drums? Find out.

Waters, Frank. *Book of the Hopi.* New York: Penguin Books, 1977. This book, like Marcel Griaule's *Conversations with Ogotemmeli,* stands as the records of peoples (the Hopi of the U.S. Southwest and the Dogon of Mali, respectively) who have come to the collective decision to reveal the secrets they carry to the world. *Book of the Hopi* reveals a worldview that ties in with all American peoples and many others throughout the world. Anyone who lives on American soil, eats American food, or has ancestors from or interest in Native America should read this book. Hopi lore resounds throughout the world. *Hetepu* means "peace and blessings, harmony" (plural) in Khamitian, and *Hopitu* means "the people of peace." Hetep.

‡Welsing, Frances Cress. *The Isis Papers: The Keys to the Colors.* Chicago: Third World Press, 1990. Dr. Welsing, a clinical psychiatrist, had to find out why her patients were bugging out. To do this, she had to answer questions such as these: Why have white people developed racism into such a science? Why are black men self-destructive? Why are golf and tennis pros nearly all Europeans, while sports like basketball, soccer, and football are so

integrated? What has this to do with drumming? Plenty. Before your spirit can be at peace, you need to see the world as more than your own. Many people dispute the Cress Theory, but it organizes the facts. *The Isis Papers* takes off the blinders; the gloves are off, too.

That's it, folks. I hope you found some things in *The Drummer's Path* that were new to you and that made it a worthwhile read. I have opened a post office box to receive responses to this book. Let me know what you think. As my teacher John used to say at the end of conversation sessions after dancing:

"Any questions? Any answers?"

God bless.

Sule Greg Wilson
P.O. Box 5643
Takoma Park, MD 20913

INDEX

Page numbers in *italics* indicate photographs.

THE DRUMMER'S PATH

AUDIOCASSETTE

AFRICAN AND DIASPORA PERCUSSIVE MUSIC

Invocation is what traditional music is all about—and what you experience in this recording. *The Drummer's Path audiocassette* is straight from tradition, with rhythms, techniques, melodies, and instruments of West, Central, South, and North Africa, from India, from South America, the Caribbean, and from the United States. This collection of sounds embodies one person's search for the root of Spirit in music, and will move you to hear the world.

Drummer, dancer, and folklorist Sule Greg Wilson studied drumming under Baba Ngoma as well as the premier students of Baba Ishanga, Ladji Camara, and Chief Bey. He has performed with many of the finest artists and groups in the field, including Babatunde Olatunji, the International Afrikan-American Ballet, Africa in Motion Dance Theater, and the Bennu Ausar Aurkestra.

SULE GREG WILSON
$9.95
ISBN 0-89281-362-8
ONE 60-MINUTE AUDIOCASSETTE

"...an offering of spirit, wealth, and journey. This book and tape are an invitation to listen in—entering when and where we can."
Bernice Johnson Reagon
Curator, Division of Community Life
Smithsonian Museum of American History

THE HEALING DRUM

AFRICAN WISDOM TEACHINGS

This intensely personal story is the first book to show the power of music as a sacred, healing force in West African culture. At a time when Africans are rapidly losing their cultural heritage to outside influences, *Lafolo Yati*—the voice of the man who speaks through the drum—tells of the depths of African spirituality and helps to preserve its timeless traditions.

BY YAYA DIALLO AND MITCHELL HALL
$12.95 PAPERBACK
ISBN 0-89281-256-7

"*...an excellent memoir...*" Mickey Hart
from *Drumming at the Edge of Magic*

"*An honest, insightful reflection on the difficulty of living between two cultures.*" *The Beat*

THE HEALING DRUM

AUDIOCASSETTE

AFRICAN CEREMONIAL AND RITUAL MUSIC

Internationally acclaimed drummer Yaya Diallo plays the sacred and celebratory music of his own Minianka tribe on traditional West African instruments. The djémbé and balafon throb with complex patterns, drawing the listener into the soul of the village, where all life flows to the beat of the drum.

YAYA DIALLO
$9.95; ONE 45-MINUTE CASSETTE
ISBN 0-89281-264-8

"*This is music that hasn't had its wings clipped; music that still possesses the full potential for the sacred and the magical that it had at the beginning of the world.*" *Magazine de la Place des Arts*

"*A music with powers to heal the troubled soul...Diallo [is] a complex fusion of old and new world thinking.*" *The Montreal Gazette*

WALKING WITH THE NIGHT

THE AFRO-CUBAN WORLD OF SANTERIA

For the first time, the secret and seductive world of Santeria is revealed by an initiate to the santeros priesthood. Seen from the inside, this little-known religion is shown to be a complex blend of African, Cuban, and Catholic mystery traditions. Canizares believes that the time has come to relax the strict code of secrecy that has cloaked Santeria's rich heritage of spirituality, in which the Divine is manifested through the medium of human beings.

BY RAUL J. CANIZARES
$12.95 ILLUSTRATED PAPERBACK
ISBN 0-89281-366-0

SACRED SOUNDS OF SANTERIA

AUDIOCASSETTE

RHYTHMS OF THE ORISHAS

Practitioners of Santeria believe that the powerful spirit forces, or orishas, provide guidance and inspiration in the form of song. The songs, chants, and drumming featured on this cassette are among the most authentic ever recorded. Side one features studio recordings made in Cuba of the most gifted Santeria soloists, choral singers, and drummers on the island, while side two contains extremely rare field recordings made in remote areas of Cuba during actual Santeria rituals in the 1940s and 1950s.

RAUL J. CANIZARES
$9.95; ONE 60-MINUTE CASSETTE
ISBN 0-89281-407-1

These and other Inner Traditions titles may be ordered directly from the publisher by sending a check or money order for the total amount, payable to Inner Traditions, plus $2.50 shipping for the first book or tape and $1.00 for each additional to:

Inner Traditions, P.O. Box 388, Rochester, VT 05767